ANGER MANAGEMENT FOR ADULTS

7 REVOLUTIONARY STRATEGIES TO MANAGE
EXPLOSIVE ANGER, IMPROVE YOUR RELATIONSHIP
WITH YOUR LOVED ONES, FORGIVE YOURSELF, AND
GET RID OF GUILT AND REGRET

ARI KOLTER

CONTENTS

JUST FOR YOU!

A FREE GIFT TO OUR READERS

9 ways to control emotional outbursts! Simply scan the QR code below or click on this link to request access to this free resource!

ABOUT THE AUTHOR

Ari Kolter is an expert in emotion management and the author of Anger Management For Adults.

Her work deals with identifying and handling difficult emotions and has grown out of the methods she's developed through working closely with clients to help them manage complex emotional challenges.

Ari holds a master's degree and specializes in helping individuals understand and manage their emotions. She has worked closely with people navigating emotional challenges for many years, and over the course of her work in this area, has developed effective ways of understanding and dealing with difficult emotions.

The emotional challenges Ari's clients face are many and varied, but anger is a common theme, and she is all too aware of the devastation this can have on a family. Encouraged by the improvements she's seen in the individuals she's worked with over the years, she is determined to share her methods of emotional mastery with a wider audience.

Ari is married with three children and two grandchildren, with whom she loves to spend her free time. She has a passion for cooking and traveling, and loves collecting new recipes from the different places she visits. She also loves singing and often lends her talents within her community..

INTRODUCTION

> *"'I lose my temper, but it's all over in a minute,' said*
> *the student. 'So is the hydrogen bomb,' I replied. 'But*
> *think of the damage it produces!'"*
>
> — GEORGE SWEETING

"Leave my store if you don't agree with the price," you yelled at another customer today.

You relegated your husband to the couch for the night because he forgot to bring you some things from the grocery store.

You came home from work stressed to meet your son playing video games when he should be doing his homework. You took his game console and smashed it on the wall, leaving it broken. You did not only break his console, but you also left his heart shattered too.

Yes, we all experience anger, being a completely normal human emotion. It can serve as a healthy measure of things that need changing in your life. At the same time, it can indicate issues that you need to address. The feeling of anger is designed to promote our survival, sharpen our focus, and keep us vigilant against threats. It motivates you to do something about emotional and physical distress, discharging tension and calming your nerves.

However, it's not all that rosy, as you already know. Many people will tell you anger is one of the most complex and powerful emotions. Zoltán Kövecses once termed anger as a "basic level" and "prototypical emotion" occupying vital importance in mapping human emotions. Like other emotions, there are different stages or intensity levels of anger. The way individuals deal with anger also differs significantly.

You often find articles online discussing waves of anger with pictures or graphics of people gesturing wildly or screaming. That is one form of anger expression. However, I want you to picture this scenario. James has spent quality time laying the right foundations for his loving relationship, which started with building a friendship with his partner, Catherine. He worked hard to have a strong friendship foundation and build mutual respect but realizes that Catherine is a person who holds in a lot of anger. Sometimes, he finds it challenging to figure out where the anger is coming from. This situation begins to take a toll on their relationship, and they eventually go their separate ways.

Anger can significantly impact relationships. Living with someone with many anger issues may cause you also to try to find fault. This is one of the most significant downsides to anger – it can be contagious, and both parties may demonstrate anger. After a while, basic feelings begin to misalign, and you start seeing your partner as someone who gets angry. This shift in thinking is the beginning of the end. Moreover, the effects of anger on children can be devastating, especially in a household of intense anger. Relationships with co-workers may also be severely compromised, affecting productivity at work.

Sadly, anger does not affect only your relationships. There are several physical effects of anger. Anger accompanies other body responses like fear and anxiety, which trigger the body's 'fight or flight' response— the result is an increase in heart rate, breathing, blood pressure, and body temperature. Left unregulated, these imbalances may cause health issues like headaches, insomnia, increased anxiety, heart attack, etc.

After an outburst, you may realize that your response was unwarranted, misdirected, or overblown. It doesn't stop there; poorly managed anger can seriously affect your self-esteem. The results are often feelings of guilt, embarrassment, shame, and remorse.

The good news? Anger does not have to take over our lives or dominate our relationships. Understanding how anger shows up in your life and recognizing the signs can help you manage it adequately. Knowing the various stages of anger and their peculiarities will also help you prevent the negative consequences. However, not many people have the luxury of this understanding, so I have come up with this book as a guide to living a better life and developing healthier relationships with others.

My desire to create a healthy living environment for people and families led me to work with people who want to control their emotions better. This raised my curiosity about anger and its effective management. I tried to tap into human psychology for several years to find the proper means to control our emotions, especially anger. The process led me to meet different kinds of people with varying levels of anger. I also discovered that only a few people have an effective means of handling their anger issues.

My desire to reach the wider world led to this ultimate guide to anger management. I learned and taught several effective anger management techniques in my years of interacting with people. I developed a program that works well for different people in managing anger and having happier and more fulfilling relationships. I congratulate you on getting this book.

The first thing I want you to know is that you are not alone. We tend to look at the most successful people in the world and can't help but notice their 'perfect' lives and relationships. But nobody is immune to the harmful effects of anger. Shia LeBeouf, the seemingly happy-go-lucky actor, has taken anger management courses due to public anger outbursts. Justin Bieber, one of America's favorites, is another example. He had to attend anger management classes in 2014 for allegedly throwing eggs at his neighbor in Calabasas. Understanding that anger affects all people, regardless of status, can help you understand that you are not alone. This understanding is the first step to over-coming the monster known as anger.

Secondly, I want you to know that there's help for you out there. There's help in this book! You can control, calm, and even eradicate your outbursts by following this ultimate guide to anger management. This book takes a whole new and fresh approach to anger, helping you understand the different categories of anger. It opens your eyes to the class you may fall into. You will learn the many things that happen in our brains during periods of anger.

Anger is a complex emotion, and linking it with your core belief can be difficult. This book aims to train your brain to change how you view the causes of your frustration, anger, and rage. It exposes you to various techniques you will not see elsewhere, showing you sure-fire ways to keep smiling instead of raging. These step-by-step helpful methods and tools will help you stop and manage these anger episodes as they arise. They give you the power to reset your mind and psychology to leave the default anger mode and channel calmness. What will you learn in this book that will open the doors to much-need healing?

Contrary to popular beliefs, anger is not the primary emotion. It is often a masked emotion, encompassing other feelings like fear, inadequacy, confusion, loneliness, hurt, etc. Anger comes to the surface when you are not in touch with your true feelings. You may not get angry when you feel guilty or inadequate. Still, you may fly off the handle in fear, loneliness, or confused situations. This book teaches you to identify and express these feelings appropriately, keeping in mind that anger arises from lacking self-awareness and self-compassion.

I remember working with an individual who got into an argument with his dad on the front porch. He swore up a storm and yelled at his dad profusely. After allowing him to vent, his dad told him, "swearing is an inarticulate and poor attempt at wanting to be heard." This book takes it a step further to prove that reacting aggressively is what the powerless resort to. You will learn to be assertive without trying to manipulate the situation in an unhealthy way. This marks the beginning of authentic living.

Mindset is a critical part of anger management. Many times, all we need to do is to shift our focus away from things that usually cause anger and toward things that make us grateful. Here, you'll learn the importance of gratitude and appreciation, helping you uncover fulfilling and satisfying experiences you may be ignoring. I like to emphasize that every event is neutral until proven otherwise. Likewise, every human's intent is innocent until proven otherwise.

Many of the events we tend to interpret as intentional are usually not meant that way. False and preconceived thoughts often lead to anger explosions in otherwise neutral (sometimes positive) events. Take this story of Anna, who always gave her husband the end piece of her baked loaf of bread. After a few months, her husband blew up in anger, demanding to know why. Anna sadly replied that it was her "favorite piece." We should never assume that we know the reasons for a person's behavior. Instead, we should learn to ask first. This book will teach you never to convict people before seeking to understand the intents or motives of their behavior.

Many of us get angry because we find it difficult to say no to ourselves and others regarding obligations and overextended commitments. Stress is a significant trigger of anger, ranging from work stress to stress from school and other responsibilities. Learning to be assertive and say no to others helps you do things that favor you, building a reservoir that allows you to help others as needed and convenient. When you have a full reservoir, you tend to feel less anger and resentment at life's responsibilities showing up from time to time. With the techniques in this book, you will learn to say no, and stick with it.

Furthermore, what you say to yourself can effectively predict how you will act in specific situations. Negative and limiting self-talk can lead you to anger reactions at the self-imposed limitations and negativity. On the other hand, positive and nurturing self-talk will reduce explosive reactions or hostile relations with others. Moreover, communication is 90% non-verbal. 55% of your communication goes into your body language, 35% to intonation, and only 10% involves actual words. This is a clean cheat sheet for communication. When your non-verbal communication does not align with your words, you are likely still upset. You may not speak a word, but your body language may communicate a billion words, showing that you still have a lot on your mind. In this book, you will learn the best means of managing your thought process and aligning your reactions (non-verbal language) with the words you use. This is key to faster anger management results.

Each chapter contains a set of exercises that will relate to the content discussed in the chapter. The exercises aim to help you understand your anger and its effects. They also assist you in applying the various techniques I will explain in this book. Yes, I know it sounds overwhelming; it's too much to take in. But knowing that there are effective ways to take control of your anger should give you a good level of fulfillment. I have only summarized the content of this book in a few words; you need to read on to discover the myriad of proven anger management techniques I have for you. I broke each of these techniques into simpler pieces, and you can be sure that you are on your way to taking control of your emotions.

While anger will remain in our lives, it doesn't have to control us. If you believe you need an emotional tuning up, perhaps this anger management guide is for you. This is the perfect investment to help you achieve the highest level of emotional mastery.

It's time to master your life! Get ready to go on a path of peace and have more beneficial, more fulfilling relationships and an overall more joyful life by adopting the techniques in this book. The approaches contained in this book have helped hundreds of people escape the confines of anger and live healthier, happier lives.

1

UNDERSTANDING YOUR ANGER

"You are not the anger: you are the awareness behind the anger. Realize this, and the anger will no longer control you."

— ECKHART TOLLE

Jake, a second-level engineer, spoke to his friend about his ongoing anger issues. After a lengthy discussion, the friend said, "Jake, you always have to express your anger to release it." Does this sound familiar to you? Many people believe that we need to vent, express, release, or unleash our anger to prevent it from becoming destructive. This myth has been around for a long time.

You hear people say things like "he unleashed his anger," as though anger was a creature he could not control. The truth is that research has consistently shown this to be a cathartic theory that does not lessen the intensity. Instead, it makes the situation even worse. We often give our anger a life of its own, creating an entity with an entirely separate mind from ours.

As you dive into this chapter, I need you to understand something that may be difficult to hear. Before you feel an emotion, there has to be a stimulus. You then translate this into the emotional response, which is anger. Your anger is your responsibility.

The key to dealing with your anger effectively is understanding how anger works. Many people tend to misunderstand the basic mechanics of anger. I will now discuss the concept of anger, explaining its stages, side effects, and potential triggers.

WHAT IS ANGER?

Anger is one of the most basic human emotions. Typically, it is a naturally occurring, sometimes unwanted, feeling triggered by other events such as emotional hurt, frustration, stress, disappointment, and many others. Some specialists define it as a dynamic state of varying intensity, ranging from mild irritation to intense rage. How we experience anger varies significantly; how often we get angry, how intensely we feel the rage, and how long the anger lasts differ for every person. Likewise, how easily we get mad and handle anger varies from person to person. Regardless of the earlier stated variations, anger is common and unavoidable.

Depending on individual situation management, anger can either be constructive or destructive. The emotion of anger signals that something isn't right in your environment. It serves as a means to survive or protect yourself from what you consider "wrong-doing." As a result, you are motivated to take action and make things right. However, allowing anger to cause you to act irrationally may have several detrimental effects on your health and relationships. It is essential to pay attention to your anger and how you react to it.

THE FOUR STAGES OF ANGER

There are four essential stages of anger, and understanding these stages will help you understand your reactions and the response of others.

The Trigger Stage

Events in the trigger phase initiate the anger cycle. These thoughts are triggered by some events in the sphere of our lives. Several things can trigger us, depending on individual experiences.

Let's go back to Jake's story before speaking to his friend. Jake was seriously bullied in his childhood. As an adult, his triggers become very intense towards anybody who attempts to control or threaten him. This becomes the initial trigger stage for Jake and a form of protection against unpleasant emotions.

While there may be several people like Jake, there are many other triggers for anger. The common ones include injustice, disrespect, abusive language and insults, physical threats, violation of personal space, lack of control, constant disappointment, misinformation, and many others. Understanding your triggers will help you anticipate your anger, making you aware of issues that alert your brain. This understanding creates a template for determining the control of the emotionally triggered response.

The Escalation Stage

In this phase, the body prepares for the looming crisis. This stage is characterized by rapid breathing, increased blood pressure and heart rate, increased muscle action, louder voice, and altered pitch. When you begin to feel any or all of these peculiar triggers, it shows that your anger is building up. Sometimes, your brows furrow, your pupils enlarge, and you demonstrate a change in body stance. See these cues as warning signs of anger-provoking conditions and work towards preventing escalation. However, you must note that these signs are not only physical or behavioral. They can also be cognitive, significantly changing your thoughts towards a person or a situation.

The Crisis Stage

Lack of proper anger management leads to the crisis stage. Survival instincts step in at this phase, and the body prepares to take action. Anger instincts impair the quality of judgment. Many times, you may make decisions without your best reasoning abilities. In severe cases, people become an extreme danger to themselves or others.

The Recovery Stage

The recovery stage occurs after the resulting actions at the crisis stage. Your body begins to recover from energy expenditure and the adrenaline rush. Your reasoning resumes alignment with better quality judgment instead of the initial survival response. Generally, there is a psychological and physiological wind-down, returning you to where you were before the triggering events. Depending on the length and intensity of the anger response, this stage may take only a few hours or could extend to several days.

After returning to a calm state, feelings of shame, guilt, and regret may follow. Some people may become apologetic to help them minimize the impacts of their behavior. Other people tend to blame someone else to make themselves feel less guilty. Many people may also feel hopeless and powerless, increasing the risks of dangerous events, such as the urge to hurt someone, suicidal attempts, and others. People also tend to be reflective in this stage, considering ways to make changes and better manage their anger.

SIDE EFFECTS OF ANGER

As I mentioned earlier, anger is not only a state of mind. It can trigger many changes in the body, both psychological and physical. During anger, the body takes about three seconds to go into complete 'fight or flight' mode. This state of mind can last up to 20 minutes each time it follows an anger response. The repetition cycle causes wear and exhaustion on our bodies, making us prone to many physical and psychological issues.

Physiological Side Effects of Anger

Remember Jake and the advice he got from his friend? Let me give you a complete view of what the advice looked like. "Jake, you always have to express your anger to release it. Keeping your anger to yourself will only make you feel more depressed. You have to vent your anger and let the person who wronged you know you were offended. You will surely feel much better after doing this." While releasing your anger is one of the best mindfulness techniques, Jake's friend did not mention the best way to do this.

Jake's issues with bullies made him very sensitive to several conditions, especially those that made him feel inferior or dominated. So, he followed his friend's advice to vent his anger, which he did in hurtful manners. A series of anger episodes led to many quarrels with his girlfriend. She eventually had to leave him when she could no longer take it. This event had several emotionally damaging consequences on Jake.

Sure, we do not always want to writhe with anger. Everyone knows that ill-managed bitterness can be unpleasant. However, many people still end up lashing out because they don't have the full realization of its potential damage to our minds. Anger puts you in a funky situation, especially at the recovery stage. You may begin to feel self-doubt, hurt, and isolation at this stage. The aftermath of your anger may lead you to push people away, even those who love and care for you the most. This resulting aftermath was the case in Jake's situation. To him, he was preventing himself from being threatened and dominated, but he was slowly pushing Rachael away.

Seeing people who love you walk away from your life is one of the most hurtful feelings. As a result, your mood worsens, adding to the feelings of guilt and isolation at the recovery stage. All of these overwhelming emotions pile up to lead to even more problems. For example, your concentration may reduce at work when doing other things. You may also have trouble managing and organizing your thoughts. Sometimes, I work with people who start to fantasize about hurting themselves and others. These are emotional and psychological consequences that arise from improper management of anger.

Physical Side Effects of Anger

Like every other strong emotion, anger causes several physical changes to the body. Not correctly addressing your anger can have significant impacts on your overall health. Let's go into a bit of science and physiology now. I mentioned earlier that anger triggers our 'fight or flight' response. Our adrenal glands release loads of stress hormones to the body during this period, including adrenaline and cortisol. Long-term activation of the body's stress response system and a consequent overexposure to adrenaline, cortisol, and other hormones may disrupt the body's processes.

Hormones work together to force blood to pump faster and harder to improve your response to anger triggers. The release of these hormones causes the brain to stop blood flow to the stomach and focus blood flow to the muscles. There is the release of glucose, supplying instant energy to these muscles. There is also the inhibition of insulin production to ensure the immediate availability of glucose for use. Furthermore, the arteries narrow, and the heart rate increases.

When you consider all these, you'll see there is no limit to the physical health damage improperly managed anger can cause. For instance, an increase in heart rate may cause palpitations, heart attacks, and stroke. During these periods, the brain shuts down digestion. Constant anger prevents the digestive tract from absorbing or digesting food properly. It is no coincidence that many people experience ulcers, abdominal pain, and digestive problems during angry moments.

Other physical effects of anger include anxiety, tingling sensations, headaches, fatigue, muscle tension and pain, weight gain, etc. Therefore, it is crucial to know healthy ways of coping with anger triggers.

UNDERLYING CAUSES OF ANGER

Anger arises due to the way we interpret and respond to specific events. As I previously stated, everyone has their own set of triggers. People interpret events differently, so something that gets you angry might not make another person angry. How you interpret triggers may depend on many factors, including:

 i. Past experiences
 ii. Childhood and upbringing
 iii. Current circumstances

Recall that Jake had a rough childhood where his peers bullied him at school for being too bright and always reading. This bullying caused him to react rather violently to his girlfriend's situation. Let's take a look at some of the potential causes of anger.

Anxiety

Many people tend to overlook the link between anxiety and anger. The more well-known anxiety symptoms are a pounding heart, clammy skin, shortness of breath, and racing thoughts. However, this condition can present itself in more subtle manners, such as frustration and anger.

Anxiety has a tight connection to overstimulation from threats or stressful environments. For instance, individuals with anxiety may find it difficult to fall asleep or stay asleep, making them sleep-deprived. Over time, such persons find it challenging to deal with perceived threats and be more sensitive to minor issues. They are frustrated over everyday events that may typically not warrant emotional reactions.

Typical examples of such situations are when you become angry in traffic, yell at a dog for barking, or get upset because there is a long line in the grocery store. Furthermore, people with anxiety disorder tend to be more rigid in their routines because they fear the unknown. Whenever something unexpectedly disrupts their routine, they often don't know how to cope with such a change properly. This disruption leads to a show of anger. For people with anxiety disorders, anger is usually an automatic reaction to long-standing effects of anxiety or anxiety triggers.

Depression

Depression is often characterized by serotonergic dysfunction – an imbalance of the neurochemicals in the brain. Depression tends to amplify negative emotions during triggering events, making it difficult to control anger. People who are depressed tend to turn their anger inward, making it hard to forget past feelings. Jake's case is the classic example here. He bottled up the bullying, leading to a critically negative inner voice and feelings of low self-esteem. This kind of anger may prolong depression or worsen the severity of the issue. On the other hand, some depressed people may turn their anger outward, taking it out on the people around them.

This condition may lead to three levels of anger, including:

▷ *Irritability*

Irritability is a characteristic of depression itself. There are no surprises to see a link between this form of anger and depression. A depressed person may snap at other people over trivial issues. They often find it hard to handle minor disappointments without responding using adverse reactions.

▷ *Hostility*

A depressed person who has an outward expression of anger may develop a hostile relationship with others. They not only respond with an irritable mood, but they are also outwardly angry, sometimes attacking people around them. This response goes a step beyond irritability.

▷ *Rage*

Depression can also lead to an intense and rapid onset of anger, also known as rage. This rage often appears out of the blue due to trivial matters. It tends to be exaggerated in relation to the actual event.

There is the possibility that your anger issue is not linked to any of the conditions listed above. I will discuss some cognitive disorders below that may relate to anger. While I will be discussing various ways to manage your anger in later parts of this book, please keep in mind that I am not a medical doctor. I advise you to speak with your doctor if you have any of these disorders and you are experiencing uncontrollable anger.

Attention Deficit Hyperactivity Disorder (ADHD)

Emotional dysregulation is one of the significant symptoms of ADHD. This condition manifests as difficulty in managing intense emotions. A substantial number of adults with ADHD often experience anger issues due to emotional dysregulation. There are often dispropor-tionate issues with anger and irritability. ADHD patients often have general difficulties with self-regula-tion, and these difficulties work in lockstep with anger. The difference in neurodevelopment may show in daily life as any of the following:

i. Feeling persistent and low-grade feelings of irritability

ii. Feeling grumpy and impatient under stress

iii. Feeling sudden anger surges, especially when frustrated in pursuit of specific goals. It could be the inability to solve a math problem or meet a significant life objective.

iv. The intense feeling of emotions, often out of proportion, leading to an explosive outburst

v. Misinterpreting other people's feelings or not noticing them at all

Obsessive-Compulsive Disorder (OCD)

OCD is characterized by cycles of intrusive thoughts and ritualistic behaviors. These behaviors can lead to an extensive array of symptoms in OCD patients. If you have OCD, you likely experience frequent bouts of rage or anger. You are not alone because studies show that over 50% of OCD patients experience anger. Anger in OCD may be a result of any or a combination of the following:

i. Constant anxiety and stress
ii. Frustrations with the disorder and its symptoms
iii. Reactions to medications
iv. Interrupted compulsions

There's usually a seemingly unending sense of uncertainty that marks OCD, with compulsions helping patients gain some understanding of control. There is always a feeling of something terrible or wrong, making OCD patients highly alert. This heightened awareness can lead to frightening episodes of anger.

Oppositional Defiant Disorder (ODD)

Like ADHD, an adult with ODD may feel angry and lose their temper more regularly. There is always a pattern of hostile, deviant, and negative behaviors, causing these individuals to argue with friends, family, and co-workers. They may also actively refuse to comply with directives to annoy other people deliberately. Sometimes, the events manifest in road rage or verbal abuse.

Adults with ODD tend to defend themselves relent-lessly whenever challenged for doing something wrong. They also constantly feel pushed around, misunder-stood, disliked, and unappreciated, seeing themselves as the victims.

Bipolar Disorder

This brain disorder leads to dramatic and unexpected mood shifts. The 'manic period' is associated with intensified feelings and euphoria. In contrast, the 'depressive period' may leave the patient sad and despairing. These mood changes in bipolar disorder come with energy changes too. Irritability usually occurs during manic periods. An irritable person gets upset quickly and often bristles at people trying to help them. They may also be easily aggravated or annoyed with requests to talk, especially if they are persistent.

Anger and Other Underlying Emotions

Anger is one of the most challenging emotions to deal with because it covers several other deep, underlying feelings. These underlying feelings serve as the triggers for anger. As I mentioned in the earlier parts of this chapter, some stimulus has to drive the emotions we feel. For anger, these underlying feelings often include fear, shame, betrayal, anxiety, stress, guilt, jealousy, hurt, sadness, shame, and several others. Before we feel an emotion, there is always a stimulus. A better understanding of these feelings will help you understand the functions of anger as a secondary emotion. This understanding is the starting point to coping with the emotion adequately.

Exercise 1

How Does My Anger Feel?

1. What is the first thing you notice in your body when you experience anger?

✎...

2. What does it feel like when your anger will "explode"?

✎...

3. What is the first thing you do when feeling angry?

✎...

4. What are the physical symptoms that characterize your anger?

✎...

✎...

✎...

Exercise 2

What is at the Root of My Anger?

1. Do you have an underlying disorder that may be contributing to your anger? If so, who do you speak to about this?

✎...

✎...

2. Thinking back on the times you felt outraged, can you think of events or actions that made you angry? List them here.

✎...

✎...

✎...

3. What are the most reoccurring events among the above-listed?

✎...

✎...

✎...

2

HOW ANGER AFFECTS YOUR FAMILY

"Anger doesn't solve anything. It builds nothing, but it can destroy everything."

— LAWRENCE DOUGLAS WILDER

The quote above is exceptionally accurate when it comes to our relationships. One of the most substantial contributors to a person's character development is family connections. . The more established a pattern is in one family, the more difficult it is to change. You may be striving to erase, understand, or copy different influences and behaviors from your family.

The various effects of anger in families are usually apparent in how the members of such families relate to one another. Anger outburst is one of the relational patterns in families, and it is likely to reappear in future relationships. Uncontrolled anger contributes to a chain reaction that may lead to the development of several unhealthy patterns and hostile attitudes in relationships. If it continues unchecked, threatening behaviors and anger episodes may escalate and have damaging consequences.

Some couples report that anger makes their relationships feel alive. The truth is that this emotion takes root in relationships where there is little to no open communication. It buries the feeling of love beneath heavy layers of resentment. Relationships where rage-filled deeds and words have overshadowed calm, open dialogues will see loving bonds among members overlayed by heavy thoughts of resentment.

With this said, I have dedicated this chapter to helping you understand the effects of anger on your family. I will explain the various ways anger can affect your children. I will also dive into the impact of anger on you and your spouse or significant other. As with the previous chapter, you will have some exercises to evaluate the effects of anger on your family.

HOW ANGER AFFECTS CHILDREN

During healthy child development, kids learn to see most people as safe and trustworthy. However, traumatic experiences such as extreme neglect, abuse, or anger outbursts may trigger intense 'fight or flight' responses in these children. The average child's brain cannot self-regulate emotions. Thus, chronic family relationship volatility may put unwanted patterns into motion. I will discuss the most common patterns you may begin to notice in your child if they have been repeatedly subjected to your anger.

Loss of Concentration

A child's mind develops as their brain responds to ongoing experiences. The cognitive pathways created by anger may translate into several emotional, behavioral, and mental patterns. One of these patterns is the lack of concentration. Many times, children tend to blame themselves whenever their parent is angry. This blame can cause a high level of stress on children, affecting their brain development. Parental anger may be in the form of verbal and emotional abuse towards a child. For example, you get home and find your child's room is untidy. Instead of calmly telling them to arrange the room, you lash out with abusive words.

Children may interpret these words differently, and they may begin to feel worthless. A child constantly at the end of their parents lashing out may lose concentration in various facets of life. Often, it appears most prominent in their school work. "What mood will Dad be in?" "Would Mom be mad at me for having a low grade?" "I got dirt on my clothes; am I in trouble?" These thoughts, and several others, come to their head every time they think of a potential interaction, and they find it difficult to pay attention. This repeated thought pattern can negatively impact them in both short-term and long-term ways.

Social and Emotional Withdrawal

You may notice that your child, who was once a social butterfly, is now becoming shy, timid, and anxious. They may appear uninterested in social events and situations. Sometimes, they may even be fearful of attending school events and hanging out with friends. Parental anger is associated with low self-image and social withdrawal. However, it doesn't end there.

Your child's time with you may reduce daily, and they tend not to share anything about their life with you. This emotional withdrawal is a significant red flag for anger issues. Children consider emotional withdrawal as a shield against perceived danger in their relationships with their parents. Some children may slowly withdraw, while others withdraw abruptly. Some of the barriers children use when emotionally withdrawn include:

1. Physical isolation (e.g., staying behind closed doors, being in separate rooms, etc.)
2. Emotional isolation (refusing to share emotional intimacy with other family members)
3. Stonewalling and hiding behind other engagements such as social media or gaming
4. Sarcasm, slammed doors, eye-rolling, etc.
5. Angry outbursts, abuse, and verbal attacks
6. Crying

Rudeness and Aggressiveness

Sometimes, children may respond to their angry parents with similar negative behaviors, including rudeness and aggression. Kids may express their frustrations through physical responses as they age. This expression often translates to poor behaviors and noncompliance. They cause frequent disruptions at home, do not follow instructions in school or act unfriendly to their peers.

Difficulty Connecting with Other Children

As I mentioned earlier, anger outbursts at home may provoke many different thoughts and feelings. One of them is the feeling of rejection when a child thinks, "my parents probably don't want me" or "could I not be their biological child?" This constant thought pattern makes them sensitive to rejection. A rejection-sensitive child finds it challenging to form new connections. They also often undermine the quality and importance of their existing relationships.

Furthermore, rejection-sensitive children may get angry and hostile at their friends for the tiniest reasons. Ultimately, such friends tend to retreat further, increasing the sense of rejection. Due to their rejection sensitivity, children subjected to parental anger may avoid relationships and other situations where they could be rejected. As a result, they may feel lonely and isolated, leading to their biggest fear coming true.

Sleeping Problems

Parental anger can also manifest issues such as nightmares and believing in monsters or fantastical beings. These combine to cause anxiety and fear during bedtime. Moreover, children carry the weight of the issues between their parents. Children may find it hard to sleep when they notice either hostility between parents or arguments close to bedtime.

Becoming Ill

Parental anger may affect a child's physical well-being, especially those translating to yelling and verbal abuse. A child subjected to constant yelling and noise may develop chronic headaches, leading to migraines and other illnesses. Some children may develop stomach issues, appetite loss, and other physical symptoms. Moreover, parental anger causes childhood stress, exposing such a child to an increased risk of potential health conditions as they grow up.

HOW ANGER AFFECTS YOUR RELATIONSHIP WITH YOUR PARTNER

"I don't have children, so my anger is not affecting anybody." If that's what's on your mind, I'd like to remind you of Jake's story. His girlfriend left him because he couldn't take control of his anger. Anger triggers many severe issues in your relationship with your partner. If not handled properly, these issues are sometimes the end of relationships.

Destroys Emotional Safety

Every functioning relationship depends on effective communication. However, the foundational element for good communication is emotional safety. I define emotional safety as trusting your partner and feeling safe with them regarding your emotional well-being. It indicates your belief that your partner cares about your emotional experience and you also care about theirs.

Every healthy relationship is built on trust. It is what makes your partner feel safe. When they trust you, they feel secure with you. Once trust is lost, relationships stop functioning in love. Among the effects of angry spouses, I find partners saying "I don't trust him..." very disturbing.

Anger is one of the most significant hurdles to couples establishing emotional safety. Often, your partner's pain may result from something you have or haven't done. It becomes difficult to hear your partner share frustrations and complaints about you because you feel like you fall short as a partner. This feeling of inadequacy makes you defensive, responding by vocalizing your complaints instead of fully listening to your partner. If you constantly explode with anger, your spouse or significant other can't believe you have their best interest at heart. This doubt changes the dynamics of your relationship since it's nearly impossible to feel safe in an angry environment. Your partner feels it's risky and unsafe to be free, open, and transparent in such situations.

Creates Rejection Sensitivity

The brain tends to store and recollect emotional pain much more effortlessly than physical pain. Take a moment and try to remember when you were physically hurt. Your brain may serve up the event's details but very few emotions. You may remember details such as the date of the event, the people around you when it happened, what happened, and your response. However, your brain won't serve up the different feelings associated with that physical pain. The opposite is the case with emotional distress because the brain is able and willing to recall all the feelings involved. It remembers feelings of isolation, rejection, and loneliness very vividly.

This vivid recollection makes anger very detrimental to relationships. It creates a sense of rejection every time your partner remembers those feelings of rejection. Your partner opened their heart to you. Thus the way you treat them affects how they feel about themselves. That is, anger may threaten their sense of belonging. It sends the message "you are not accepted the way you are," making your partner feel rejected. When your partner develops rejection sensitivity, it does not only affect them in the relationship but also in their daily lives. They constantly expect to be rejected, often acting in ways that push others away. They anxiously hunt for evidence that someone doesn't want to be with them.

This behavior sets in motion a painful cycle that is difficult to interrupt. People who suffer from rejection sensitivity may see rejection as confirmation that they are in some manner unacceptably flawed. Rejection is viewed as a verdict on their worth and value. This belief system can be harmful in relationships. It's challenging to feel safe in a relationship when one expects rejection. Even if they aren't being rejected right now, they are constantly on the lookout for it and expect it to happen at any moment. As a result, minor blunders are interpreted as a complete lack of concern. They may also translate it as scathing assessments of their worth as a person. Finally, when a rejection-sensitive person perceives a prospective rejection, they most often respond with worry and anger.

Creates Distrust

It is not wise to undervalue the importance of trust in your relationships. It plays the principal role in developing a cooperative relationship between you and your partner. Anger is the ultimate killer of trust, and it breeds discontent in a relationship. It takes time for a person to develop a sense of distrust. It progresses through stages, and if you can recognize these stages in your partner, intervention before doubt takes hold is possible.

▷ *Doubt*

Doubt is the first step in the distrust process. Your partner begins to have a nagging doubt about your trustworthiness, which prompts them to halt for a moment. It could be the nagging doubt in the back of their mind that they can't seem to dismiss. It could also be that something about the circumstance doesn't feel right, even if they can't point it out exactly.

▷ *Suspicion*

Something is wrong, according to your partner's trust radar. It is based on a lack of evidence. Your partner notices a conduct pattern that could indicate a lack of trust. Still, they don't have enough evidence to draw a definitive conclusion. Unresolved doubt develops into suspicion.

▷ *Anxiety*

Anxiety, a sensation of apprehension or uneasiness frequently reflected physically, is the third stage of distrust. Your partner may begin to feel uneasy, have a racing heart, be angry, have a knotted stomach, or even be disgusted when interacting with you.

▷ *Fear*

When fear is reached, the level of distrust in your relationship has escalated to a point where your partner is afraid to express vulnerability. They've been the victim of repeated betrayals of trust, and they've learned to distrust you to the point where they're concerned for their emotional well-being.

Your partner enters a condition of self-protection due to fear. They begin to build barriers in their connections to keep you from getting too close. This effort of self-preservation decreases their vulnerability and cements distrust.

▷ *Withdrawal*

Loneliness, as well as a sense of being dead or frozen on the inside, is prevalent. Rather than acting carefree as they would normally do, your partner becomes more cautious about disclosing personal information. Because the safety net of the relationship has been withdrawn, they stop taking risks in the relationship.

Trust holds two people in a relationship together, and anger can seriously damage it. When severed, disconnection becomes the order of the day. This disconnect was the case with Jake and his girlfriend. She didn't just leave him all of a sudden. Jake's constant anger episodes gave her several reasons not to trust her boyfriend anymore, which led to her total withdrawal from the relationship.

Creates Distance and Builds Walls

Have you ever heard the term 'Porcupine Effect?" Some people also call it the hedgehog's dilemma. Here's a picture to help you understand it. On this cold night, a group of porcupines desired to remain warm, so they decided to help each other by coming together. As they moved closer, their sharp spines began to stick to each other's bodies, and they could not accomplish their goal of warmth. This was their dilemma. The same is the case with anger in relationships. While you and your partner desire value, acceptance, and intimacy, anger is the sharp porcupine spine that hinders everything. It pushes your significant other away, preventing you from getting what you want out of the relationship.

These are some of the features you may see in your spouse when they are emotionally distant:

i. Low self-esteem
ii. Exhibiting poor listening skills
iii. Having difficulties opening-up
iv. Experiencing a lack of physical, verbal, and sexual contact
v. Having contradictory ideas about you

When there is emotional distancing or barriers between you and your partner, the results can become hurtful. One person may begin to become critical of the other person. This criticism leads to further withdrawal, causing more distress and criticism.

Causes Unfaithfulness

People may consider cheating out of anger or the desire for vengeance. Perhaps you've recently found your partner has been cheating on you. This betrayal takes you a step back, and you are hurt. You could want to have your spouse experience the same emotions as you to ensure that they truly comprehend the harm they've caused you. In other words, retaliatory infidelity is frequently motivated by the thinking, "They hurt me, so now I'll do the same." However, this is not the case for every relationship. Although I am not condoning unfaithfulness, the temptation may occur when anger pushes your spouse away.

Consider this. When do you feel the most vulnerable to any temptation? When you're feeling lonely, isolated, and unaccepted. Does this sound correct? When your partner repeatedly conveys the message (via their anger) that you don't measure up, you begin to seek different ways of feeling better about yourself. Moreover, the feeling of loneliness due to unmet needs may cause your spouse to think of seeking satisfaction elsewhere.

Loneliness

The level of satisfaction in a relationship is determined by how respected, and free (secure and protected) the partner feels. This concept ties together with the two previous points I made. Emotional satisfaction is low when unresolved anger lowers emotional stability and a partner's sense of worth. It causes anxiety and loneliness. Your partner may feel pushed out when you are angry. It makes them feel like they've lost touch with their source of acceptance and love.

Now that you know the various ways your anger may be affecting your life and your relationships, you may be wondering, now what? That's where my seven effective techniques come in. I will break down these techniques into easily discernable chapters to help you understand how to get hold of your anger. Before we get into that, don't forget to complete the exercises below.

Exercise 1

Times I Have Felt...

Here, I will mention some ways anger can affect you in a relationship, and I would like you to write about times you have felt these things. Let's go!

Rejection

✎...

Loneliness

✎...

Doubt

✎...

Distrust

✎...

Unwanted

✎...

Fear

✎...

Withdrawal

✎...

Vulnerable to Temptation

✎...

Others

✎...

Exercise 2

Times You Have Felt...

This time, get your partner to complete this exercise, talking about times they've felt the following emotions.

Rejection

✎...

Loneliness

✎...

Doubt

✎...

Distrust

✎...

Unwanted

✎...

Fear

✎...

Withdrawal

✎...

Vulnerable to Temptation

✎...

Others

✎...

3

#1 LOOK AT YOUR LIFESTYLE

"Health is a state of complete harmony of the body, mind, and spirit. When one is free from physical disabilities and mental distractions, the gates of the soul open."

— B.K.S, IYENGAR

The previous two chapters exposed you to the concept of anger and how it can affect you and your relationships. You likely agree that anger is one of the mental distractions that could prevent the soul's gates from opening. Failure to properly manage your anger could cause health problems, threats to your spouse and co-workers, and social and emotional hazards to your children. It could also leave you wasting time being upset about unnecessary things.

Managing your anger does not necessarily mean that you will never get angry. I mentioned earlier in this book that anger can be a good emotion in certain situations. However, it is crucial to recognize and cope with your anger. You must also know how to express anger in healthy and productive ways. Every person can learn anger management. Even when you've tried various means to control your anger, there's always a step further.

As promised, I will be discussing seven ultimate anger management techniques for adults in this book. This chapter focuses on one of the essential techniques—lifestyle changes. While anger is a secondary emotion based on other underlying emotions, lifestyle choices may also determine how effectively you can control your anger. Some of the things we do affect how quickly we get angry and how easily we can maintain the anger. Read on to see how your lifestyle may be affecting your anger and the various changes you need to make for proper anger management.

SPEND LESS TIME ON SOCIAL MEDIA

I'm discussing this topic first because hardly any adult out there doesn't use social media, ranging from Twitter to Instagram, Facebook, TikTok, etc. The truth is that most people don't understand the dangers involved in overindulgence in social media.

Picture this. It's a bright Saturday. Your day is going as planned since you have paid bills, run your errands, done grocery shopping, and are ready to spend some time with your family. You hear a notification beep on your phone as you are driving home. While stopping at the red traffic light, you check to see that it is a Facebook alert notifying you that a "friend" replied to something you posted earlier about updating the local movie theater.

While this is a positive post, the replier attacks the post, accusing the country of wasting money on unnecessary constructions instead of helping the homeless. Your mood changes, your face turns red instantly, and before you realize it, you pull over, ready to defend your stance. After that, you put your phone down, drive home, carry that anger with you throughout the day and even share it with others.

That's not you? Let's see another illustration.

The week has been crappy. Your bathroom pipes broke today, and your hallway flooded. You got into a fight with your wife earlier about the cat overeating human food. Your son is being bullied at school, and you have to see the school principal tomorrow. Don't forget the vet appointment and your hallway carpet that needs shampooing. With these in your head, you are trying to get some sleep. Then, you notice the myriad of Instagram notifications on your phone. You scroll through them only to see happy faces, job promotions, and new home purchases. You put off your phone angrily, feeling worse about your week and thinking why you couldn't have such a 'perfect' life.

Social media users have quadrupled in the last five to six years with no indication of slowing down. Many people acknowledge social media problems like false lives, tunnel syndrome, manipulation, and addiction. The growing anger is something people don't talk about as much. There is a barrage of information on the internet and the introduction to several different people whose life is portrayed in a particular way on social media. This trend already makes us feel average, unhealthy, or like losers, creating pressure and anxiety in many people's lives.

There's a desperate and constant feeling to defend yourself on social media. There's always this feeling of having a void that needs filling in your life. Social media creates an unnecessary self-consciousness, making you feel like you're not good enough regardless of how hard you try. There's a desperation to keep up, catch up, and pay up, causing people to pack their phones at the hip. All these create a wave of underlying anger.

As with everything else, moderation and responsible use of social media is crucial. Social media doesn't only create anger towards others; it can often make you angry at yourself. To minimize the negative impacts of social media, spend less time on social media and thus decrease the level of comparison and self-shaming.

STOP BINGE-WATCHING TV

We are in the streaming era, and this is changing how everyone watches television. These days, you don't have to wait a long time for new episodes of your favorite TV shows. Entertainment companies now release entire series and seasons at once, leading to the concept of binge-watching. Remember Jake's childhood, where he was bullied and was always alone with no friends. He got used to this lonely lifestyle and saw binge-watching as a way to escape from the 'ever-dangerous' world. Little did Jake know that binge-watching TV was doing him more harm than good.

Social Isolation

If you binge-watch TV shows, there's a high probability that you do so in solitude. Therefore, the more you binge-watch, the more you isolate yourself. Behavioral studies report links between binge-watching, social isolation, and poor mental health. Shutting the world out and being on your own for a prolonged time can lead to loneliness. Prolonged loneliness may further progress to depression, physical fatigue, and other anger triggers. It can also affect personal relationships and work responsibilities as you tend to neglect these things when you begin to "binge" on an engaging show.

Sleep Problems and Fatigue

Sleep plays a significant role in your physical and mental well-being and overall quality of life. I will discuss the connections between sleep and anger in the latter parts of this chapter. However, you must note that sleep is crucial for adequate brain functioning and promoting physical health. Binge-watching TV is connected to sleep deficiency and increased fatigue. You may find it more difficult to fall asleep at the proper time, and you start to feel sleepy closer to morning. Lack of sleep affects total mental and physical health and a loss of productivity. All of these are triggers for anger.

The End of the Show May Leave You Feeling Let Down

While you may be enjoying yourself when binge-watching a TV show, it will inevitably end. At this point, you may feel significantly let down. You find yourself responding to TV characters like they were your actual friends or acquaintances, missing them when they are gone. You get angry at the ones that hurt your "friends," investing so much into the meanings created by the storylines and their exciting events. By the time everything's over, you are back to the dull reality of life, which is not so great for your mood.

Now that you know how bad binge-watching TV can be for your mood, you also need to learn how to break this habit. I helped Jake understand that watching TV should be an occasional pleasure, not something he should do every day. It would help if you understood the importance of this, and I believe the following tips will help you do so effectively.

Limit Yourself

It would be best to watch the episodes in bits. For example, you can choose to watch two episodes of your show at a time. Once you complete the two episodes, turn off your TV and do something else.

1. **Set a Time Limit.** Choose an appropriate amount of time to watch the television. It could be two to three hours every evening. Set the alarm to keep you on course.
2. **Find a Balance.** Balance watching TV with other activities such as reading, exercise, spending time with your family and friends, etc.
3. **Make TV Watching a Social Activity.** You can use TV watching to socialize with friends, co-workers, or family. If you have someone else coming over to watch with you, you will limit how much time you will spend watching.
4. **Have a Bedtime.** Binge-watching TV typically causes you to sacrifice several hours of sleep. Therefore, it would help to have a bedtime alarm to keep track of time.
5. **Snack Healthy.** Many people tend to munch on unhealthy snacks while binge-watching TV. It would be best to choose nutritionally dense snacks. Dump the salty, fatty snacks for fruits and vegetables.

While there's nothing wrong with enjoying catching up with your favorite TV show or series, you must do it in moderation. When you begin to have problems with responsibilities, ignore other activities, and spend lesser time with friends and family, your TV time may be a serious problem. The above-listed strategies can significantly decrease the adverse effects of excessive TV viewing.

EAT HEALTHIER

The famous saying "you are what you eat" may be right. Growing research results reveal that what we eat may significantly affect how angry we feel. For instance, a study showed that diets high in trans fatty acids are linked to increased aggression. The trans-fatty acids interfere with the production of other nutrients that help lower aggression. A deficiency of such nutrients as Omega 3 fatty acid exposes one to risks of depression and may contribute to irritability.

Enough of the science; let's dive into the relatable part. It is not only the things you eat that can make you angry; what you don't eat can also provoke anger responses. Hungry people are more prone to aggressive reactions. The hungrier a person becomes, the lower their blood sugar level falls and the angrier they tend to be. It is no surprise that the saying, "a hungry man is an angry man," is popular. The question now is, what food can help you with anger management??

You don't have to overhaul your diet to get your desired result. A few modifications to what you already have will do the trick. A meal that contains complex carbo-hydrates, some proteins, and fruits is the best choice for improving your mood. Serotonin is a feel-good chemical that helps to improve your mood. Complex carbohydrates from complete foods like rolled oats, sweet potatoes, legumes, and quinoa can increase the availability of serotonin in the brain.

You also want to load your plate with plenty of dopamine-rich foods. Such foods include eggs, fish, and leafy greens. Foods rich in omega-3 fatty acids would be great options because they help ward off feelings of depression. Examples of such foods include flaxseed, walnuts, fish, and chia seeds. Sprinkle in some magnesium-building foods to improve your sleep. They include almonds, pumpkin seeds, sunflower seeds, and spinach. Since low vitamin D levels are associated with mood disorders. You also want to eat enough egg yolks, liver, and fatty fish to get optimal vitamin D levels.

Meanwhile, you want to avoid foods that can cause mental drainage. Some foods have low nutritional values and may lower your energy levels and mood in the long run. I recommend avoiding flour-based foods like bread, baked foods, and crackers. Sugar-added varieties or sugar-sweetened snacks and beverages are also not great options. Overall, keep in mind that balance is vital.

CURB THE DRINKING

Rational thinking, judgment, and impulse control are crucial in keeping emotions in check. However, alcohol lowers or seriously impairs these factors. It only takes about two drinks (blood alcohol concentration of 0.05) to impair cognitive functioning. This decline also begins the early phase of alcoholic rage. Aside from limiting a person's ability to think straight, alcohol also narrows attention span.

When drunk, you may miss environmental and social cues to help you rationally interpret situations. This means that you tend to take the bait whenever someone provokes you when the proper thing to do is to think of the consequences. This lapse in rational thinking may lead to angry or violent reactions to the slightest offenses. Moreover, alcohol consumption is associated with heightened stress responses and increased cortisol levels. Stress and related hormones are already top triggers for angry responses.

There is also a direct correlation between aggression and testosterone, the hormone that diminishes impulse control and cognition. It also reduces your sensitivity to fear and punishment. Thus, you are more likely to be aggressive due to a lack of fear of repercussions. Alcohol also decreases inhibition, which can be very harmful if you've been suppressing your anger for a long time. Alcohol consumption may trigger anger responses and physical violence in some cases. Similarly, alcohol can enhance the natural disposition of people with inherent anger.

Therefore, the optimal option is to stay away from alcohol or reduce it to the barest minimum. Doing this will significantly help you progress with your anger management.

STOP SMOKING

There's a likelihood that you started smoking because of your anger issues. I've seen many people do this, and a classic case was Jake. Aside from preferring his 'alone-time,' he often smoked to calm himself. He didn't know that the nicotine present in the cigarette caused brain activities that further triggered his aggressive behaviors.

Experts link chronic marijuana smoking with changes in the brain cortex. This brain region regulates reactions to behaviors and emotional control. Changes in the activity of the cortex can lead to bursts of rage, anger, and aggression, especially in those prone to irritation. Some who suffer from anger gradually turn from strictly smoking tobacco to smoking marijuana.

How did Jake get over his smoking addiction? Trust me; it wasn't easy at first. He would stop, then go back to it, then stop again. However, he could get hold of himself using the following tips that you can also implement:

1. **Prepare for the Change** — Think about your smoking experience, and write down what you will gain if you stop smoking. These include better health, improved concentration, fresher breath, and more productive spending habits.

2. **Get Support from Friends and Family** — Trying to quit smoking will be much easier with support from family and friends. Tell your family members and your friends to discourage you from smoking whenever you try to. They can also help keep cigarettes, lighters, and ashtrays away from your reach.

3. **Avoid Smoking Triggers** — Learn to know why you smoke and when you crave smoking. It could be after a meal or at a party. You want to avoid these situations as much as possible. Most cravings last only a few minutes. Your ability to ride the cravings out will put you closer to quitting smoking for good.

4. **Find Other Means of Coping with Stress** — If smoking is your coping mechanism for stress,

you need to find more productive ways to deal with it. Breathing exercises, meditations, regular exercise, a balanced diet, etc., may be helpful. Talking to a friend about your stress can also help.

5. **Don't Give Up Even if You Relapse** — You may relapse in your quitting journey and want to go back to it. Don't let that put you off from trying again. Use that opportunity to think back on why you wanted to try again and what went wrong. This will help you learn more about yourself, and you can figure out what will help you going forward.

Smoking was one of the major causes of the fights between Jake and his girlfriend. The techniques above helped Jake quit smoking altogether. They played a significant role in his future, which I will get to later. I firmly believe they will help you too.

MAKE SLEEP A PRIORITY

While anger may stem from several sources, many of which have already been discussed, lack of quality sleep is one factor that many people don't acknowledge. Lacking adequate sleep intensifies the feeling of anger and other similar troubling emotions. Not prioritizing sleep is among the worst choices you can make if you want to regulate your emotions. If you struggle to keep your anger in check and maintain a positive attitude, trace back to see if you lack sleep.

Poor sleep quality and duration increase negative emotions like depression and stress. This correlation is especially the case if you experience constant daily fatigue. Stress is a significant trigger for anger, so the reason is not far-fetched. Getting a recommended amount of sleep will help you in your anger management journey. Take a moment to gauge your sleeping patterns and ask yourself, "Is there something I can do to improve my sleep pattern and quality of sleep?"

Again, lifestyle changes will help make that big difference in your sleep, health, and emotions. The following tips will help.

1. Set a sleep routine, including a consistent bedtime and wake-up time
2. Eat a healthier diet consisting of plenty of magnesium.
3. Avoid stimulants such as coffee close to bedtime.
4. Get regular exercise
5. Turn your electronic devices off at least 30 minutes before bedtime. You could also wear

blue-light-blocking glasses if you have to use electronics.

6. Meditation and music are alternative ways to sleep better, especially when stressed.

LISTEN TO MUSIC

Over the years, I've discovered that incorporating music into the anger management process is very effective. One reason is that I believe music will help you recall incidents that impact your life, allowing you to reflect on the positive aspects. Music can help you put many things into new perspectives. Depending on the type of music you listen to, you may find a story you can relate to or significance in the lyrics. When it comes to anger, I tell the people I work with to choose songs with a similar story to the situations they experience. This synchronicity will help sort through angry feelings constructively. This way, healthy anger will replace destructive or violent outbursts.

While I usually recommend calm, slow-tempo music to relax your muscles and quiet your mind, having a personal preference will also work. Different types of music have different effects on people. Some people find classical, instrumental, or spiritual music more soothing to their senses. Others claim angst-ridden lyrics make them calmer. Regardless of your choice, listening to your favorite songs can:

1. Lower your heart rate and stress levels
2. Release 'feel-good' hormones and improve your sense of well-being
3. Distract you, reducing your emotional and physical stress levels

Sometimes, performing music, either privately or publicly, can assist your anger management. You may even try to compose song lyrics to express your deep-rooted feelings of anger or anxiety. Subsequently, using music as a constructive outlet proves to be an excellent way to cope.

CUT OUT CAFFEINE

For many, coffee starts their day; it is that much-need eye-opener or can serve as a pleasant break after work. The caffeine in coffee helps you remain alert and reduces fatigue. However, excess caffeine consumption can be dangerous to your physical and emotional health. Irritability and anxiety are significant draw-backs of caffeine consumption. Caffeine intake may aggravate your anger, depending on the amount you take. Reaching out for your coffee cup every moment of the day may cause some noticeable physiological or mood changes.

As we previously discussed, lack of proper sleep can negatively impact your mood. Drinking coffee or soft drinks too close to bedtime, or taking too much caffeine throughout the day, may significantly degrade sleep quality. To minimize caffeine interrupting your sleep, drink your final caffeinated beverage of the day at least four hours before bedtime. Although drinking coffee before bed won't make you upset, you might be irritable the next day if you had a restless night's sleep.

Caffeine is contained in various consumables, including coffee, caffeinated tea, cocoa, chocolate, and sodas. Consuming over 500 milligrams of caffeine (over four cups of coffee daily) can cause mood changes, including anger. Caffeine can be found in several pain medications, cold treatments, and hunger suppressants. If you need to reduce your caffeine intake, do it gradually over a few days or weeks. For example, if you're having withdrawal symptoms, try cutting back on your coffee intake by one cup per day or even less and advance as tolerated.

EXERCISE REGULARLY

Anger often occurs due to frustration and anxiety redirected towards others. Exercise is one great lifestyle choice that can reduce irritation resulting from frustration. It helps burn off excess energy and release powerful endorphins that improve mood. Increased blood pressure can also be a trigger for anger. And as I mentioned in chapter 1, high blood pressure is one of the physiological effects of excessive anger. Exercise helps to reduce your blood pressure, regardless of its cause.

You may have difficulty giving your energy to workouts, especially when anger consumes you. However, I will group the exercises you can do into some exciting categories. Jake particularly liked the first category because he could do it in conjunction with listening to his favorite music.

Sweat it Out

Aerobic exercise is a type of exercise that involves energy use and is usually done for several minutes or longer. Aerobic exercise, sometimes known as cardio, refers to various routines that increase your heart rate. Aerobic exercise reduces blood pressure and relieves stress by boosting heart rate and exercising the pulmonary system. You may consider exercises like:

1. Boxing
2. Jumping rope
3. Circuit training
4. Jogging
5. Bicycling

"Ohm," it Out

Mind-body exercises like yoga have proven effective in lowering blood pressure, improving mood, and decreasing anxiety. If there is any way to remain calm when angry, yoga and other mind soothing exercises may just be the best option. The exercises you can do here include:

1. Yoga
2. Tai Chi
3. Meditation

Walk it Out

Walking has several health benefits, including heart health and reducing the risks of some diseases. Walking is an excellent means of releasing anger and helping calmly cope with anger triggers. I suggest trying the following:

1. Walking
2. Hiking

Groove it Out

Dance is one of the best ways to demonstrate joy, and it also helps express emotion and dissipate anger. Dance movement therapy can address depression, fear, and even rage. There are other ways to move and groove your body with rhythm, breath, and affirmations. They include the following:

1. Meditative movements
2. Expressive dancing

Try to stay open-minded, trying various exercises from the above. Note that the goal of the exercise is not necessarily to eliminate your anger. It simply provides an outlet to help you express and effectively manage your anger.

I implore you to look back at your lifestyle and check what needs changing. This reflection will set the pace for your anger management. Besides lifestyle changes, being aware of our triggers is another crucial aspect of managing our anger. I will discuss this extensively in the next chapter. Before moving on, don't forget to complete the exercises below.

<u>Exercise 1</u>

How My Lifestyle Affects My Anger

1. Do you drink or smoke often?

✎...

2. Does your drinking or smoking cause disagreements with others?

✎...

3. What are the activities you do when you are at home?

✎...

4. Do you prefer to stay binge-watching movies indoors or go outside for some exercise?

✎...

<u>Exercise 2</u>

The Changes I Can Make

What are things I can change about my lifestyle?

✎...

How will these changes affect my anger?

✎...

#2 IDENTIFY TRIGGERS

"We cannot control what emotions or circumstances we will experience next, but we can choose how we will respond to them."

— GARY ZUKAV

I know that "triggered" seems like a buzzword. I was recently in an elementary school, and I heard a child that appeared to be around eight years old saying they were "triggered" by something their friend said. I couldn't help but giggle a little while at the same time realizing maybe we're raising more emotionally aware humans than our parents did.

Although your lifestyle can be the primary reason for your anger issues, it is also essential to identify your triggers. You don't experience the same feelings as your friend, family member, or spouse. While these feelings seem more substantial than the cause or appear to surface from nowhere, they can be due to triggers. The emotions are proportionate, and they have logical causes.

Identifying your triggers is a complex process because of the numerous types of triggers. However, this does not mean that it is entirely impossible to identify those areas that cause an immediate physical response for you. Knowing your triggers will help you predict anger responses and react appropriately.

With that being said, I have devoted this chapter to helping you identify your triggers. I will explain the meaning of triggers and dive into the various things that may trigger your anger. I will also explain how you can identify and manage emotional triggers.

WHAT ARE TRIGGERS?

Triggers refer to anything that affects a person's emotional state by causing extreme distress or over-whelming feelings. They often bring up different thought patterns, influencing your behaviors and affecting your ability to remain in the moment. Triggers can also be anything that causes a flashback or strikes your memory, taking you back to the event or trauma. It can be in the form of emotional distress, panic attacks or flashbacks, etc. They are physical or emotional reactions that remind you of a traumatic event that occurred in the past. Triggers are activated by one or all five sense organs: eyes, nose, skin, tongue, and ears. The most common sense organs to quickly trigger a person are the eyes, ears, skin, and nose, with the tongue as the last. Although the trigger varies, there is a common theme:

Eye

1. The object that the abuser used to carry out the abuse
2. The environment the abuse took place (i.e., a specific place in the house, family gatherings, or holiday)
3. Someone who has similar traits or resembles the abuser (i.e., walking pattern, hair color, or clothing)
4. A situation where another person is being abused (it could even be a verbal comment to accentuate physical abuse.)
5. Object relating to or shared in the environment where the abuse took place.

Nose

1. Any form of smell where the abuse took place (it can be an odor, food cooking, or even the scent of wood)
2. Any scent that resembles that of the abuser (perfume, drugs, alcohol, or tobacco)

Ear

1. Any sound relating to fear or pain (i.e., screaming, whispering, or crying)
2. Abusive words (or could be a curse word, put-downs, labels, or a word the abuser used)
3. Any sound relating to the one made by the abuser (whistling, tone of voice, footsteps)
4. Any sound present on the day of the abuse or one that reminds of the trauma (sirens, music, chirping, or yelling)

Skin

1. Anything that looks like the abuse or things that occurred before and after the abuse (it could be physical touch, the way someone approaches you, petting an animal, a person standing too close)

Taste

1. Any taste relating to the abuse, before or after the abuse (i.e., a particular food, tobacco, or alcohol)

Triggers can come from undeniable traumatic events like war or sexual violence. They can also come from micro-trauma. In micro-trauma, hurt and pain build up over time. People tend to sweep these kinds of pain and hurt under the rug because they seem minute. However, you do not wish for these feelings, whether the triggers are micro or from a life-threatening situation. You tend to be lost in the moment, and you may react inappropriately.

WHAT TRIGGERS ANGER?

Several things can trigger you to get angry. Here are some of the everyday things that can cause instantly heightened emotions:

Unfair Treatment

You are bound to be mistreated at one time or another. You may feel enraged, irritated, or even annoyed when something unjust happens to you. Here are typical examples of unfair treatment:

1. A police officer punishes you when you know you did not commit any offense
2. Your boss gives an incomplete evaluation of your work
3. A teacher gives you an unjust grade
4. Someone cuts in front of you at the bank or in line at the movies

No matter your reaction to an unjust situation, the most important thing is whether your response was productive, in line with the problem, or blown out of proportion.

Getting Attacked

Violence pervades the world. A victim of abuse or violence can have naturally occurring feelings of anger. Some victims also respond with depression and anxiety. Abuse comes in different forms ranging from mild to blatant. In some cases where a person was severely abused, they can also become an abuser to express the pent-up anger and victimization they carry with them.

These are various categories of attack or abuse:

1. Domestic or partnership physical violence
2. Domestic or partnership verbal abuse
3. Child abuse
4. Sexual abuse or rape

5. Battery and assault
6. Genocide
7. Verbal intimidation
8. War trauma
9. Random accidents and violence

As with prejudice and discrimination, you may be the victim or the perpetrator. Both involve a substantial amount of anger. For example, Jake was bullied as a child, and he grew to become an angry man, always having a reason to pick a quarrel with different people. Are you the victim or the perpetrator? Examine yourself to know which one you are. In rare cases, you may be both the victim and the perpetrator.

Prejudice and Discrimination

Some people who face prejudice and discrimination see themselves as powerless, and they feel they cannot change their world. They respond with rage, anger, despair, or even irritation. The cause of prejudice and discrimination can be mild or blatant. Anger can be triggered by being prejudiced or intolerant or being a victim of intolerance and bigotry. The list of common prejudice is endless. These acts could be due to nationalism, sexism, classism, religious and racial differences, disabilities, sexual orientation, etc. Some even prejudge based on media exploitation and bias.

Reactions to Frustrations and Time Pressure

The world is a hectic place. You often feel the need to multi-task consistently to increase your work output. But as with any situation, there is likely to be an unforeseen obstacle requiring you to refocus energy. This disruption hinders your work and may get you annoyed. You could wake up late for work only to find yourself in a traffic jam. Security personnel may pick you up for extra screening even when running late for a flight. Your son keeps calling to ask for some money when you are busy with work. It could be anything, and these events can be very frustrating. However, you should note that it can happen to anyone, and these events are liable to happen no matter what we do to prevent them. Getting angry over these issues won't help the situation. Instead, it will add to your stress.

Experiencing Disappointment or Dishonesty

When people lie to you, break a promise or let you down, it is customary to get annoyed or upset. Several things could make you feel disappointed. It is down to you to recognize these things and handle them accordingly. It could be something as simple as your best friend forgetting your birthday and something as serious as your partner cheating on you. I once was displeased with my coworker for making up a lie to escape from work. Another coworker of mine expressed frustration when our boss told her she would get a raise and then did not follow through during annual evaluations. Disappointment is inevitable, and how we choose to react will make a world of difference in the outcome.

Facing a Threat to Self Esteem

It is human nature always to want to feel good. Even people with low self-esteem don't want to experience criticism and put-downs. Some people tend to react to threats to their self-esteem by being sad or self-loathing. However, many people respond by getting angry. Examples of threats to self-esteem are:

1. Losing an election
2. Getting rejected
3. Receiving a bad report or evaluation
4. Making mistakes in public
5. Getting disrespected or insulted
6. Spilling wine on someone's dress
7. Not being selected for a sports team

IDENTIFYING YOUR TRIGGERS

Identifying triggers requires effort and practice. There are, however, specific measures you may follow to get started on recognizing triggers in your life. Remember that while you might only have one trigger, it is not uncommon for people to have many distinct triggers. Irrespective of its kind or source, recognizing the trigger is the first thing toward obtaining help. You can identify your triggers by following these four basic steps.

Identify Your Response

It isn't easy to pinpoint a trigger, but it's a lot easier to assess how you're feeling at a specific moment. Take account of what you're going through when feeling overwhelmed by strong emotions. Are you enraged, unhappy, or envious? What about bodily indicators — does your heart race? Do you breathe quickly? etc. It will be more straightforward to identify the triggering incident if you examine your feelings (both physically and psychologically).

Reconsider Your Steps

After analyzing your feelings, try to recall what brought you to the situation. Was there any specific point when you realized you were experiencing destructive emotions? What were you up to before you became agitated? Try to think about the problem and what exactly made you angry. Because triggers are frequently founded in previous traumas and experiences, it's okay if the triggering occasion doesn't "make sense." Perhaps you were going to work and had a flashback to a casualty. It can be anything, so try to figure out what made you upset in the first place.

Rerun the Cycle

Don't get disheartened if you can't find a trigger during the first attempt at the exercise. These emotions are frequently complex, and it is not a sign of failure if it takes several efforts to identify a psychological trigger. Many people become discouraged, but remember that you can recognize these feelings even if they do not occur immediately. Repeat the exercise until you can identify commonalities in events, emotions, or even particular people involved each time you feel the trigger happening.

Keep a Trigger Journal

Prevention is the best medicine. Being able to anticipate scenarios will help keep your anger in check. You can opt to avoid stimulating circumstances altogether. If that isn't possible, you can prepare strategies to reduce the risk of losing control before entering potentially risky scenarios.

An anger diary or journal can be a helpful tool for keeping track of your angry experiences. Make regular entries in your journal to record the incidents that have triggered you. There are specific types of information you'll want to note for each inciting occurrence to optimize the value of the journal. Some of the questions you will want to answer are:

1. What happened that caused you to be in pain or stressed? What or who provoked the situation?
2. What were the ideas that ran through your head?
3. How enraged were you? (Rage Level: 1-10) What impact did your actions have on you and other people?
4. Were you already apprehensive, tense, and under pressure from another situation?
5. What was your body's reaction?
6. Did you notice your palms sweating and your heart racing?
7. Was your head aching?
8. Did you want to run away from the stress or throw something? Did you yell, or did you catch yourself slamming doors or being sarcastic?
9. How did you feel right after the emotion subsided?
10. Did you have a different feeling later that day or the next? What were the ramifications of the incident?

After about one week of recording this material, review your diary and look for recurring themes or "triggers" that irritated you. I recommend classifying these triggers into various categories, including:

1. People are taking advantage of your vulnerability to self-defeating thoughts and anger
2. Situational occurrences that come in your way, such as traffic jams, computer problems, ringing telephones, etc.
3. A combination of any of the above

It will help if you repeatedly keep an eye out for anger-inducing thoughts. You'll know these thoughts since they usually revolve around one or more of the following topics:

1. The belief that you have been wronged or victimized
2. The view that the person who provoked you intended to harm you
3. The belief that the other person did something wrong, that they should have acted differently, that they were evil or stupid for causing you damage

Use your rage journal to track times when you felt harmed, why you thought the act was done on purpose, and why you felt it was wrong. Tracking your thought patterns will assist you in identifying recurring themes in your life. To get you started, here are some examples of trigger thoughts:

1. People are unconcerned about you
2. People expect/demand too much from you
3. People are obnoxious or uncaring
4. People take advantage of you or use you.
5. People are self-centered; they only care about themselves
6. You are criticized, shamed, or disrespected by others
7. People can be cruel or mean
8. People are either dumb or incompetent
9. People are irresponsible and careless
10. People are not willing to assist you
11. People are slackers who fail to do their part

The idea that people are misbehaving and that you have every right to be upset with them is the root of many trigger thoughts. The majority of people have a few ideas that frequently make them angry. Look for scenarios that make you mad and see if you can pinpoint the specific collection of triggering thoughts that precede the situation. Your diary's objective is to assist you in identifying patterns of behavior and specific repeating factors that "press your buttons." The more accurately you can watch your feelings and behaviors, the more complete your anger diary is, and the more likely you recognize anger triggers and responses.

MANAGING EMOTIONAL TRIGGER

Since triggers can come up at any time, you need a long-term strategy to deal with them. Here are a few tips for managing your emotional trigger:

Be Mindful

Being present means being mindful. Pay attention to your emotions and remain in the present. Use mental preparation tactics to get mentally ready. It's simpler to recognize your triggers and cope with them. From childhood to adulthood, self-regulation is vital. If daily meditation and yoga are beneficial, then engage in these activities regularly. Jake was able to control his response because he knew his triggers and was able to practice mindfulness. This did not come easily or quickly for Jake, but he was able to eventually take control of his own emotions through the practice of mindfulness.

Know When a Relationship is Toxic

A toxic relationship is one where there is a lack of mutual understanding, respect, and consideration. Some people will disturb and annoy you regularly. Even if you beg them respectfully to stop, they will not comply. This is an example of a toxic relationship and one that will not serve to benefit you in any way.

Change Your Notion About the Trauma

Trauma has a long-term psychological impact on how we think about other people, the world, and ourselves. Our brain needs to comprehend the danger. It frequently gives us emotional "short-cut" explanations that allow us to bury the pain deep into our subconscious. "No one can be trusted" or "I make lousy decisions" are two common explanations.

You may grow distrustful of others and yourself due to these trauma-related thoughts. When awful things happen, you may begin to blame yourself, dwelling on how you "could or should have" done something differently. With ideas like, "If the person I used to trust could injure me so horribly, why can't this person?" You may begin to think that everyone has a hidden agenda. Your nervous system can become locked on high alert if you hold on to these ideas without addressing their emotions, resulting in an inability to relax, increased

social isolation, restless sleep, and strained relationships.

Despite being victims of discrimination and prejudice,
historical figures like Nelson Mandela and Gandhi
channeled their rage and anger into exceptional works
and life-changing movements. Therefore, you must
learn to see your current situation as something
designed to make you a more robust, better person.
Stop seeing everyone as a threat to your security, and
start creating space for self-development and healthier
relationships.

Seek Professional Help

Emotional self-regulation is a difficult skill to master.
Self-regulation is taught to young children as early as
possible so that they can adapt and adjust as they grow
older. Triggers are frequently so profoundly embedded
in a person's conduct that they cannot notice them. If
you're having trouble identifying your triggers, I
encourage you to seek professional help. Therapy is a
confidential, judgment-free environment where you
can explore your triggers. While healing, therapy can
provide you with support and educated guidance.

Exercise 1

My Triggers

Circle any of the following that often triggers your anger:

- People being nosy or asking rude questions
- Messy neighbors or family members
- Crowded stores or public transport
- Traffic
- Poor working conditions
- Waiting too long in lines
- Places that bring back bad memories
- Hunger, loneliness, or fatigue
- Being wrongly accused
- Rumors and gossips
- Slow customer service
- Being lost in an unfamiliar environment
- Losing an item

Exercise 2

My Trigger Journal

Create a trigger journal, answering the questions stated above in the Trigger Journal section.

...

✎...

✎...

✎...

✎...

✎...

✎...

✎...

✎...

✎...

✎...

✎...

✎...

✎...

✎...

✎...

✎...

✎...

5

#3 BE MINDFUL

"We cannot become what we want by remaining what we are."

— MAX DEPREE

You have already made up your mind to manage your anger better. You've examined your lifestyle to see changes you need to make while keeping tabs on your triggers. The next step is to make conscious efforts to understand who you are, as Max Depree's quote above suggested. Being mindful of yourself is another vital step towards getting hold of your anger. In this chapter, I will discuss the concept of mindfulness and how you can use simple mindfulness exercises to get the best out of your anger management journey.

WHAT DOES IT MEAN TO BE MINDFUL?

Being mindful has always been part of your everyday life and activities. You are usually conscious of time, language, where you put your hands, how much you spend, etc. The meaning of mindfulness in daily life is closely related to paying attention to the different activities you do. For example, you have to catch a plane at noon, so you have to be especially aware of the time that morning. Or you have your monthly performance review coming up, so you need to pay close attention to every detail of your work. It could also be that you are on a diet or watching your weight, so you remain vigilant about what you eat.

The situation is the same when we talk about mindfulness related to your anger. Mindfulness is your ability to be fully present and aware of where you are and what you are doing. It is a time-to-time awareness of your feelings, thoughts, bodily sensations, and environment. At the same time, you are not being overwhelmed or reactive by the things around you.

Being mindful also means accepting your feelings and thoughts without judging them. You acknowledge that there is no "wrong" or "right" way to feel or think in certain situations. When you are mindful, your thoughts will tune into what you're feeling in the present. You won't find yourself reviewing the past or imagining the future.

When angry, you may notice that you often divert from the impending matter. Your mind tends to take flight, making you lose touch with your body. In no time, you start becoming engrossed in raging thoughts about what just happened, or you are worried about what might happen. However, mindfulness is always there to snap you back to where you are, regardless of how far you drift away. Mindfulness exercises, such as the ones I will discuss soon, will help you reduce stress. They will also help you gain awareness and enhance your judgment of situations through proper observations. These proven techniques will help calm your anger, returning you to the present moment.

MINDFUL EXERCISES TO HELP MANAGE ANGER

Mindfulness practices are vital in understanding and overcoming anger. These exercises will guide you on the path to adequate anger management. You will work towards overcoming anger and recognizing these feel-ings for what they are. Let's get into the exercises.

Recognize, Realize, and Breathe

This exercise is on top of my list because I believe it is the primary technique for becoming mindful. The first step to dealing with your anger is recognizing its pres-ence inside you. While this may be challenging in times of anger, it lessens the impact of the anger. If you try to resist or suppress anger, it will only increase your nega-tive feelings and anxiety.

Next, you have to realize that anger is normal. When you can't properly control your rage, you tend to hurt yourself, as I established in the earlier chapters of this book. Also, you have to admit that you are deserving of all the love in the world, especially your own love. A simple realization that anger is completely normal is a huge step towards your progress.

There is a phrase I always love to tell people I work with, and I'll share it with you too. "When you are in doubt, return to your breath." This technique has proven very effective over the years. I firmly believe it is one of the most potent mindfulness exercises. Breathe in, knowing that a feeling of anger has mani-fested in you. Then breathe out, smiling towards your anger. Doing this does not imply suppression or fighting. It is an extension of recognizing your anger and embracing it with awareness and tenderness. The idea behind this exercise is to reverse some physical symptoms of anger. Whenever you start to feel angry or tensed, isolate yourself for a few minutes, then concentrate on steady, calm, and relaxing breathing:

1. Inhale and exhale 4 or 5 times deeply in a row
2. Count slowly to five as you inhale
3. Count slowly to ten as you exhale
4. Focus on the air that moves in and out of your lungs
5. Feel how your ribs slowly rise and fall as you breathe
6. If you begin to feel dizzy at any point, stop and go back to normal breathing

Use Your Senses

Anxiety and stress have significant links to anger, as you may already know. The pressure you experience daily can be exhausting. Fortunately, using your five central senses can bring you back to where you want to be. The following is a 5-sense grounding exercise for anger management.

▷ *Sight: 5 Things You Can See*

Look around for five different things you can see in your environment. Notice their shapes, colors, shadow, light, etc. Describe these things in as much detail as you can. For example, when I direct my attention to what I see inside my office, I see a ceramic vase and stacks of books of different sizes on my desk. I also see yellow flowers, my coffee mug, and a penholder my daughter made.

▷ *Sound: 4 Things You Can Hear*

Do the same as you did above, but this time, close your eyes. Focus your attention on four different sounds you can identify and try to describe them in detail. In this case, you may need to slow down to notice quiet and subtle sounds. For instance, I can hear the clicking sound of my keyboard as I type, and this sound quickens and slows down sporadically. Next, I can listen to my coworker guiding her mouse across her desk, cars zooming by and honking outside, and the ceiling fan blowing above me.

▷ *Touch: 3 Things You Can Touch*

Use your physical sense of touch to interact with your environment in three ways. It could be as simple as noticing the cool air on your cheeks or feeling your bottom pressed into a chair. In my case, I can feel my feet pressed firmly against the wood floor. I can also feel how smooth my keyboard is and the grooves with each key. Lastly, I feel my back pressing against my leather chair, eliciting comfort.

▷ Smell: 2 Things You Can Smell

Check for two things that you can smell. It could be the smell of your deodorant or the freshly mowed grass in your yard. I can smell the lovely scent of my perfume left on my hoodie from when I last wore it. As I raise my mug close to my mouth, I perceive my coffee's sweet and intense aroma; this smell comforts me.

▷ Taste: 1 Thing You Can Taste

Look around to see if there's something around you that you can safely put in your mouth. If there's food or drink nearby, you should try that. If not, you can notice the taste already present inside your mouth. My mouth is full of ripe strawberries, sweet chocolate granola, and vanilla yogurt because that was what I had for break-fast. The burst of chocolate awakens my taste buds with the subtle yogurt taste countering it. It feels so lovely and sets my mood up for a great day.

If you were following, how did it go? Were you able to complete the five senses countdown exercise? I'm hoping you feel relaxed after and have felt your stress decrease.

Count to Calm

As a kid, I remember how my mom used to put us out in a timeout for inappropriate behaviors and asked us to count to 10. The actual counting process aimed to calm her mind and body, preventing her from lashing out in anger. It also prevented her from saying something harsh to us. This brings me to my third mindfulness exercise, which I tag 'count to calm.' Some people may refer to it as calming counts.

Calming breath and natural breathing are two components of calming counts that might help you access the calming response. In this exercise, instead of paying attention to your worrying thoughts, you'll spend that time focusing on another specific activity — counting. You'll give yourself 90 seconds to relax your body and clear your mind. During these 90 seconds, you will count from 1 to 90 in approximately one-second intervals. This exercise allows for engagement of the mind while also allowing time to pass, thus providing both your body and mind with the required rest.

The fight-or-flight stress response is countered by deep breathing. Taking a slow, deep breath relaxes you and focuses your mind on the moment. Anger's "energy" frequently leads to rash behavior that escalates an already difficult situation. You can learn to manage your early lashing out by giving yourself sufficient time to cool down.

Here's a simple way to go about counting to calm:

1. Sit comfortably.
2. Take a deep, long breath and exhale slowly. You could say the word "relax" silently in the process.
3. Close your eyes.
4. Allow yourself to take ten easy, natural breaths.
5. Count down as you exhale with each breath. I recommend starting with the number "ten."
6. If you notice any tension in parts of your body during the comfortable breathing, imagine them loosening up.
7. Open your eyes when you reach number "one."

Counting from one to ten is an old calming technique that works for most people. Jake shared his experience with me, using the method differently. He found this 'count to calm' exercise very effective in keeping him calm. The twist he added to the exercise was that he always counted from one to ten, getting better results. I took his suggestion and recommended it to many other people who reported more powerful effects using this technique.

Use Mantras

Several people looking for 'control' tend to use different mantras. However, using mantras is not about control. They involve recognizing and accepting that we might not have control over certain situations. While we cannot control many of our thoughts, we can control our awareness and responses to problems. Mantras are navigational tools to help you sail the stormy seas of life, work, and everything related. It involves words, prayers, or chants, often repeated for concentration. You can call it a form of truism. Mantras facilitate a deep understanding of your anger and how to respond to it.

I find the following mantras most effective for anger control:

"This, too, shall pass, and I can do this."

Diverting your thoughts from the person(s) or the situation(s) is the most efficient way to deal with anger. When anger comes knocking, repeat, "This, too, shall pass, and I can do this." Close your eyes gently and repeat this mantra until you feel a sense of peace in your heart. Also, recite this mantra to keep yourself calm and free from negativity. This chant can end rage and keep the body and mind at ease. Take a deep breath and tell yourself that you are capable of accomplishing everything you choose.

"I breathe in calmness and exhale toxicity."

When you're stressed or anxious, the best thing you can do is breathe in and breathe out. This is one of my favorite mantras, and I do it even when I don't feel angry. Not only should you chant the mantra, but you should also follow it. Inhale deeply while reciting, "I breath in calmness." Hold your breath and think of anything pleasant that makes you smile. Make sure your negative thoughts are replaced with good ones. As you exhale, recite "I exhale toxicity." Repeat this mantra and breathing cycle until you feel a shift in your energy and mood.

"It is what it is!"

There are two kinds of scenarios: those you can control and those you cannot control. I recommend that you assess the situation and take appropriate action. Concentrate on what you can manage and leave the out-of-control issues alone. Recite "it is what it is" to remind yourself that you have no control over the circumstance and can't do anything about it. The ability to accept situations is a positive state of mind; accept the things you cannot change and move on!

"Nobody can disturb the peace of my body and mind."

Once you've mastered the skill of detachment, the next step is to avoid being sidetracked by negative energy. By silently, or out loud, repeating "Nobody can disturb the peace of my body and mind," you are taking back your power and emotional control. Repeat this mantra whenever you feel stressed or anxious, and watch how quickly the stress and anxiety vanish!

"Let it go!"

Have you seen the movie Frozen? "Let it go," with solid lyrics by Idina Menzel, is one of the most motivational songs in the film. The song's lyrics are motivating, and this was my inspiration for this mantra. Inhale slowly and deeply while thinking about what triggered your anger. As you exhale, repeat, "Let it go." Repeat this mantra until you feel calm. This mantra is very effective because it helps you first recognize the cause of your anger. Then it teaches you to let go of the negative emotion. Instead of harboring it inside you and allowing it to develop, you learn to release the thoughts and move on with your peaceful life.

Practice Meditation

Meditation is the practice of fixating your attention on a specific thing, be it breathing, sound, movement, an object, or a sensation. The popular opinion is that meditation helps you empty or quiet your mind. However, I believe it is more about teaching your mind to focus. You guide yourself towards balancing your nervous system and keeping it calm. As I have said many times, daily stress can affect your thoughts and emotions, keeping you in negative ruminations. Regular meditations can help refocus your mind and calm your body. Practicing meditation can also reduce the scattered feelings and thoughts while restricting the impulses to act on those thoughts.

I will discuss some meditation exercises that have proven effective for anger control. I recommend that you do them in a quiet place while closing your eyes or gazing at an object. You may choose to meditate while sitting or lying down, especially when at home. Breath deeply and slowly, and repeat your favorite meditation as many times as you may need to calm yourself. Here are four practical meditation exercises for anger management.

▷ *Watch Your Breath; Let it Lead You.*

You already know how crucial your breath is for anger control and mindfulness exercises. Let your breath take the lead in this meditation, and give your emotions and thoughts a rest. The relaxing rhythm of your breath helps you to release tension and anger from your mind and body. Allow yourself to connect with the part of you that isn't angry. Meditate through the following steps:

1. Inhale deeply and slowly, imagining a soothing light mixing with your breath's fresh air and filling your body.
2. Hold your breath for about two seconds, allowing it to gather feelings of anger and tension.
3. Exhale slowly and comprehensively, visualizing the feelings of anger and tension leaving your body.
4. Feel your body relax as you exhale.
5. Repeat this meditation until you feel centered and calm.

▷ *Release Anger From Your Body*

This meditation concentrates on physical feelings and any stress you may have in your body. Anger manifests itself in our minds, emotions, and physical bodies. Focusing on the bodily manifestations of anger may help you become more aware of where you're keeping your anger and allow you to release it intentionally.

Carefully follow these steps:

1. Breathe and focus on your feet while wiggling your toes and flexing your feet; imagine your feet muscles letting go of the anger
2. Direct the attention towards your legs; check to see if there are knots or tightness
3. Squeeze your leg muscles, imagining them releasing the anger
4. Repeat the same step for your arms and hands; you can clench your fingers to make fists and release them gently, picturing anger running off your body
5. As you breathe in, visualize a gentle wave moving through your chest, washing off the anger and tension
6. Move your neck gently to release knots of anger
7. Don't forget the muscles on your face; scrunch them to dissipate the anger and tension
8. Scan your body again from toe to head, attend to and release any lingering feelings of anger and tension

▷ *Observe Neutrally*

Practice observing your emotions and thoughts in this meditation, expanding your awareness and allowing them to exist without judgment. Examine your thoughts and shift your focus from these thoughts. Try to see whether your urge to react (based on these thoughts) changes.

The following steps will be helpful:

1. Focus on something specific; it could be a sound or an object you like.
2. Take note of the sensory details, including sound, texture, shape, color, and sensations it gives your body.
3. Notice whenever your mind wanders off and gently bring it back to the sound or object.
4. Stay in those emotions and note how your body is responding.
5. Remain in this experience and resist the urge to act on any rising feelings; let them flow out of your focus as you gradually go back to the object or sound of your focus.
6. Repeat this cycle until you feel calm.

▷ Boost Self-Regulation

Self-regulation or self-discipline is one trait many people tend to lose when angry, and it is usually hard to draw back on its strengths. Follow this meditation to bring self-regulation back to the forefront of your attention:

1. Breathe in, say, "I am in control."
2. Breathe out, say, "I release my impulsive desires."
3. Breathe in, say, "I am stronger than the anger feeling."
4. Breathe out, say, "I slip out of the grasp of anger."
5. Breathe in, say, "I am in control."
6. Breathe out slowly and completely

▷ Try Candle Gazing

As the name suggests, this is a mindfulness exercise that involves you gazing at a candle flame. Several people, like Jake, find this exercise relatively more straightforward than using mantras. Others find it a bit challenging, sometimes tricky, to focus their eyes on a candle without blinking. However, you will become more comfortable with this open-eye meditation when you practice it for some time. One sure thing is that it will improve your focus and help you find a relaxed state of mind. Here's how to do candle gazing effectively:

1. Find the best time of the day for you.
2. Settle in a dark, quiet space without interruptions.
3. Sit straight and comfortably, with the candle at your eye level.
4. Take some deep breaths and settle into your focus.
5. Set a timer for one minute.
6. Follow the candle flame's movement with your eyes.
7. Observe as your thoughts begin to come up; gently let the thoughts go without judging or engaging with them.
8. Try not to blink as you go through this exercise.
9. End the exercise with gratitude to yourself for connecting to the light within.

These mindfulness exercises are effective, and they help you understand yourself, your emotions, and the best ways to react. Getting to this stage marks significant progress in your anger management journey. Being mindful can help you calm yourself in a moment of stress. Still, you need to deal with underlying issues causing you anger so that you can stop it from manifesting. I will discuss this extensively in the next chapter. But before then, don't forget to take the simple exercise below:

Exercise 1

Try It

Carefully review the mindfulness strategies I discussed in this chapter and pick the one you feel would be most comfortable for you. Reflect on the outcome of the process, stating below how you feel after completing it.

✎...

✎...

✎...

6

#4 DEAL WITH UNDERLYING ISSUES

"Identify your problems but give your power and energy to solutions."

— TONY ROBBINS

When it comes to our anger, we all need to be detectives to determine its underlying causes. Many people suffering from anger issues, anxiety, depression, or a combination usually find themselves at a crossroads. Whenever we go through challenging situations, we often find it hard to think clearly. It is normal to feel out of sorts and overwhelmed in these conditions. As adults, the inability to address these issues may increase their intensity because the under-lying issues get pushed to the subconscious mind. Here, they cycle repeatedly, causing constant episodes of distress as we try to keep them away from our consciousness.

This chapter discusses the common problems that lead to anger and how you can overcome these issues. Let's get right into it!

THE DIFFERENT EMOTIONS AT PLAY

Sadness

You can feel sad for several reasons. It could be that you lost something or someone significant. It could also be that something didn't come your way. Sadness ampli-fies negative emotions, making it difficult to control anger. Sad people sometimes turn their anger inward, making it difficult to forget past feelings. Some people turn their anger outward, taking it out on the people around them. He bottled up the bullying in Jake's case, leading to a critically negative inner sense of low self-esteem. This kind of anger may prolong sadness or worsen the severity of the issue.

Sadness may lead to irritability. A sad person may snap at other people over trivial issues. It is usually quite difficult for such persons to handle minor disappointments without responding using adverse reactions. Sadness may also cause a person to be hostile. A person who expresses their anger outwardly may begin to have adversarial relationships with other people around them. Sometimes, you find such people attacking others. In that case, they begin to show signs of the rapid and intense onset of anger — rage. The feeling of rage may appear out of the blue and could be exaggerated, depending on the event.

How to Deal with Sadness

One common way many people try to deal with their sadness is by avoiding it or judging themselves for feeling the emotion. However, judging or burying your feelings is often ineffective in dealing with anger. The following healthy strategies will help you convey and address this feeling:

- *Acknowledge Your Feeling*

The first thing to do is understand that it's okay to feel sad sometimes and that you're not alone in the struggle. Don't hold in your sadness and pretend that you're okay. Instead, you must own up to that feeling. Doing this makes it much easier to release the sad emotions and heal faster. It also helps you get the best support you need. At this point, if someone asks you how you are feeling, be honest and tell them, "I'm sad." If opening up to someone else feels like too much at this point, tell yourself. You can look into the mirror and admit your feelings by stating, "I'm sad." You can also choose to write down the feeling in a journal.

- *Allow Yourself to be Sad*

It's not productive to chastise or beat yourself up for being sad. Give yourself that space and time to live in the emotion without criticizing or judging yourself for it. Do what you have to do and let the sadness out. It is okay to cry a bit, lie in your bed, or even snuggle up with your favorite pet. However, do not wallow too long in sadness. Set a deadline for yourself; one or two days (depending on the situation). After this period, get ready to change your mood with activities you enjoy.

- *Prioritize Personal Care*

There are simple activities that can help you overcome your sadness. They all center around taking time to care for yourself. Channel that feeling of despair into creative expressions. It can be by writing stories, songs, or poetry. You can also paint or draw something that helps you release the feelings in the best way possible.

Don't sit around doing nothing. Push yourself to get up and move around.

Physical activity stimulates the release of endorphins, the 'feel-good' chemicals for your brain. Walk around and play with your pet, organize a private party with your best friend, or do something else you enjoy. However, it would be best to avoid unhealthy coping such as taking drugs, alcohol, or consuming junk food. While these activities may numb your pain, it is only temporary. Self-care and positive activities are the best choices in these situations.

- *Stay Connected with Other People*

When you're upset, turn to your friends and family for support and encouragement. Simply having someone there for you can be beneficial. Isolating yourself will only exacerbate your feelings and cause you to dwell on your sadness. Joining a support group is also very effective for dealing with sadness. Participating in a face-to-face or online support group is a fantastic opportunity to meet new people and get assistance. This way, you can discuss your emotions with other people who can relate and empathize with you.

Betrayal

Betrayal is one of the most painful losses a person can suffer. Before betrayal can occur, you must have first trusted the person involved. If you didn't trust the person in the first place, it's nearly impossible for you to feel betrayed. The term "betrayal," as used in this book, may relate to different forms. When a child is being abused by the people supposed to love and protect them, such a child is betrayed. When a spouse's partner has an affair, they are betrayed. When someone you trust cheats on you, lies to you, or abuses you, this is betrayal.

When the betrayal and loss are fully realized, you will likely become enraged. This is a critical stage because many things can go wrong at this point. Many people's natural reaction to being betrayed is to react with anger, retaliating, and hurting the person involved.

How to Deal with Betrayal

While it is normal to feel betrayed, it's preferable not to react immediately. However, this doesn't mean you have to stay completely blind to the situation. Take time to go through all phases of grief before deciding how to respond. Even if it takes a few weeks to work through the process, it is better to wait than regret hasty decisions. Here are six practical steps to help you heal from a betrayal.

- *Personal Reflection*

Once the dust has cleared, and the emotions aren't quite as raw, you can benefit from a good reflection. This is a moment to examine yourself and comprehend the betrayal, its aftermath, and the long-term implications in your life. You may wish to evaluate how you can try to prevent similar circumstances in the future by reflecting on your immediate thoughts, feelings, and behaviors following the betrayal.

Reflect, but try to make it as productive as possible. Ensure that it doesn't linger too long and strive to move past the betrayal. You will need to deal with any intrusive thoughts you have regarding the act of betrayal. After all, you're bound to have many questions about what occurred, how, and why. However, constantly thinking about these issues will keep you in the emotionally tricky state of mind you're currently in. Stick to inquiries about yourself and how you can deal with the betrayal; it'll be easier to discover answers to those.

- *Be Realistic About the Current Relationship*

You may find yourself reminiscing about the beautiful times you had with the betrayer in the past. However, you must try to avoid this as much as possible. Accept that your relationship had problems before the betrayal, and be realistic about it. Being realistic will open your eyes to the difficult time you had in the relationship before the betrayal occurred. Doing this will help ease the feeling because you won't feel like you've given up the "perfect life" with such a person.

- *Allow Yourself to Grieve*

Grieving is an essential part of getting over what happened. In some circumstances, this may imply mourning the end of a relationship. It could also mean mourning the future you had envisioned for yourself and the other person. Anger and despair will undoubtedly be present, but so will various other emotions. You may even experience a brief period of depression. Instead of repressing your feelings, feel them. You'll have to face the fact that what happened did happen. This is the best way to acknowledge the pain caused by the betrayal.

- *Consider Forgiving the Betrayer*

Strive to have the spirit of forgiveness, even if it feels impossible at that moment. Forgiveness is for you, not for those who betray you. Forgiving someone does not imply that you approve of what they did; instead, it means that you seek to let go of the pain associated with it. Forgiveness means that you conclude that it is better to move on from the hurt than to allow it to consume you and affect your relationship with the other person. It also encourages you to let go of any resentment toward the person who betrayed you. You'll eventually be able to put that betrayal behind you, even if it's just for the most part. You may never be able to let go of it entirely, but it will no longer have a significant impact on your life. It will require effort, and it will not always be easy, but you'll get the hang of it with time.

- *Take Care of Yourself*

I have probably mentioned taking care of yourself too many times in the book. But the truth is that I cannot overstate the importance of self-care. Treating your mind and body with kindness helps you heal faster. As with the case of sadness, you should get regular exercise, get proper sleep, and spend time doing things you love. These activities will improve your overall outlook on the situation and about yourself.

- *Get Help*

Once you figure out that it is difficult for you to move beyond the thoughts and pain of betrayal, it may be that you have developed betrayal trauma. This can happen in different kinds of betrayals, but it is most common during childhood or a betrayal involving infidelity. If you notice a change in behaviors and consequent issues with your day-to-day life, you may need help from professionals. There is no shame in seeking outside assistance to process complex emotional situations. Joining a support group is also a great option here.

Fear

Fear is a solid unpleasant emotion that occurs due to awareness or anticipation of danger. Things that connect anger and fear are purpose, control, regrets, and conflict. The primary reason behind people's fear is that they have lost control of circumstances, individuals, or situations. A lot of people consider anger as a way of gaining power. While a fearful person may decide to hide the cause of their unrest, an angry person will use their displeasure to counterbalance the source of their fears.

Anger acts like a motivational force to strike back at someone or something. Many people see fear as weakness, so they use anger to show strength.

Conflict can breed anger, fear, or both, like purpose and control. Conflict is a common occurrence, and it can occur on various occasions. Physical confrontation and verbal arguments are conflicts that can arise. Threats can also be made from a place of fear, anger, or both. A person facing threats is usually prone to experiencing anger. It can be challenging to know whether fear or anger is appropriate in times of conflict. Regret also connects anger and fear, and this feeling surfaces after a particular outrage or fear-induced incident. You may fear losing someone you love after shouting at them during an episode of rage.

How to Deal With Fear?

There are four basic steps to deal with your fears, they are:

- *Learn About Your Fears*

Learning about your fears is the first step toward dealing with them. It can be challenging, but this step is crucial. Whenever you look at a person, you observe how the person acts and what the person looks like. Examining your fears will also give an insight into what they look like. To face your anxiety and fears, you can keep a journal for two to three weeks and write down any noticeable patterns. Ask questions like; when do my fears arise? Do I experience it more at night or in the morning? What are the common causes? How do I usually respond to these fears? Getting answers to these questions can help you understand your fears better. At this point, they do not seem so big anymore, and you can easily find solutions to them.

- *Have A Positive Imagination*

Imagination is a beautiful thing. It allows you to be creative, gives you power, and helps you think outside the box. However, active imagination can be dangerous when it leads you to believe negatively. Your imagination can expand your fears, making them more complex than they should be. Instead of letting your imagination magnify your concerns, you can purposely use it to overcome your fears.

How can you do this? Choose a quiet time when you're not anxious but relatively relaxed. Then close your eyes, and imagine that you are in a situation that makes you scared. If you are someone like Jake, the imagination will be that you are being bullied. Now, imagine handling that situation peacefully. Search for the correct information, regain a sense of direction, and gently leave the fearful situation. In the case of Jake, he imagined standing up for himself, being assertive, and ultimately preventing the bullying. The peace of mind you experience in that scenario can be helpful when the actual situation comes up.

- *Concentrate on Your Breathing*

If you carefully followed me through the previous chapter, you will agree that breathing is essential for anger management. Anxiety and fear often start with a short breath. Short breathing produces different reactions in the body, leading to an anxiety attack. The best way to avoid such attacks is by controlling your breathing. Luckily for you, deep breathing is relatively straightforward. The moment you realize you're getting fearful, focus on your breathing. Try taking a deep breath in and slowly breathing out. Make sure you exhale more profoundly than you inhale. Deep breathing will guide your body into a state of physical calmness.

- *Practice Mindfulness*

You may think to yourself, mindfulness again? Yes, it is that important! Being mindful is an excellent way of overcoming your fear. It is a versatile technique that makes you aware of yourself and your emotions. When you identify your fear, think about the whole situation first. Fear may get you engrossed in raging thoughts. However, mindfulness will snap you back to the present, regardless of how far you have drifted away. Mindfulness exercises, such as the ones I discussed in the previous chapter, will help you prevent unproductive fear. Precise observations will help you gain awareness and enhance your judgment.

Hurt

At a point in everyone's life, we experience emotional pain, sometimes unavoidable. When things do not go as expected, you get frustrated, resentful, and hold grudges. All of these emotions revolve around feelings of hurt. Unaddressed pain can turn into anger. For example, you can get hurt if your partner says something awful to you. If you do not deal with that pain, you will get angry whenever you remember the occurrence.

Traumatic experiences can control your brain and make you feel like you can't control your emotions. Traumatic events have a way of lasting longer in the memory. Some memories may be connected to unpleasant occurrences such as fear, terror, etc. Anger may come in to make you feel in control and safe about the situation. If your anger is related to a traumatic event that happened in the past, you may have to address the hurt. I will discuss the best ways to deal with the hurt below.

How to Deal With Hurt

There are three primary ways to deal with hurt, they include:

- *Make Positive Emotional Changes*

The first step is to accept and acknowledge that you've been hurt. Understand your pain and define it; don't let it define you. It may be challenging to accept, but it will help you heal. You can take a few minutes of your time to breathe and think about your feelings without you trying to analyze them. Name your emotions, which will help you differentiate yourself from those feelings.

You should also understand that it is okay to grieve. If you have experienced any form of hurt, you need time to feel angry, frustrated, and sad. You may go through these for months, depending on what happened. Gaining control over your emotions is also very crucial. You may not be able to change how you feel after a hurtful situation, but you can manage the feelings.

If you don't make every effort to control emotions, they'll be in charge of your life. You can do some relaxation exercises like yoga whenever you feel angry. You can also divert your attention from the situation by traveling, visiting the gym, etc. Remember to never dwell on the past. Agree that you have been hurt and believe that you do not have to feel sad anymore since the situation is over. Do not let the hurt define who you are; permit yourself to move on. An excellent way to avoid dwelling on the past is by talking to someone you trust about your emotions.

- *Practice Positive Thinking*

Learn to think positively. Remember that you are not damaged; you are valuable and worthy no matter what has happened to you. Appreciate the good things in your life, regardless of how little they seem. Also, you must do away with negative thoughts. Engaging yourself with negativity can bring you down. If you find yourself thinking about something negative, try to change it to positive. Surround yourself with positive, happy people. These people can be your friends, family, or co-workers, anybody that makes you comfortable and gives you a positive vibe. Being around such people can have a profound impact on healing.

- *Learn to Rebuild*

Here, you are taking responsibility for your actions. If you are partly responsible for what happened to you, see it as an opportunity to learn and grow. Experience is the best teacher; you shouldn't feel embarrassed about it. Take a look at your mistakes and see how you can learn from them. You should also share your story with a trustworthy person. Whenever you share your problems with someone you trust, you'll realize that the burden will be eased. Sharing your stories allows you to understand your situation better. What seems like a big issue may not be that serious.

LEARNING TO LET GO

Why do you find it hard to let go of the past? Why can't you let go of memories and experiences that caused you so much pain? Many people find it hard to let go because of the need for certainty. Letting go means that you forget things of the past and focus on the present realities. You may also find it challenging to let go of the past if you don't link emotions and information appropriately. Let's take, for instance, a woman with a deep feminine core. If her partner causes her emotional pain, she may bring it up throughout the relationship. The partner may feel that he cannot make her forget the issue no matter what he does. She then continues to punish him for his past mistakes. Read on to learn the most effective ways of letting go and living a more fulfilled life.

Five Ways to Let Go of the Past

1. Learn to Forgive Past Events

The first thing to do is find out what may be holding you back and why you need to move on. Why are you holding on to a failed relationship? Why are you still communicating with someone that gives you pain? When you figure out what's wrong, you can look for ways to move forward. You may need to forgive someone for you to let go of anger and be more peaceful with yourself. The next thing is to discover your purpose, allowing you to establish your goals. The emotional drive will be your purpose whenever you feel like giving up. If your goal is strong enough to drive you, you will remain dedicated and focused.

2. Know Your Emotional Habits

The most challenging phase of letting go is identifying your emotional habit. It requires you to take a bold step. How do you live emotionally? Do you have limiting beliefs? When you get used to living with some emotions, you won't know when they begin to affect your life. You won't know you're stuck in an emotional loop with deceitful thoughts and that you're reacting the right way to the situation. Your unique emotional habit will be helpful in how you move on from the past and how you design your lifestyle from there.

Knowing your emotional habits will help you see the positive side of life. You can train yourself not to feel stressed, depressed, or frustrated after a challenging situation. You can also train yourself to always look at the brighter side and choose continued happiness when bad things happen. When you fall into a harmful emotional habit, work towards cutting off the thought and try to switch gears immediately. The more you condition yourself, the more wired your emotions become, and the more you adapt to different situations.

3. Control Your Mind

Changing your habits requires your mind to be in the right state. If you don't take charge of your mind, you open yourself to illusion, negativity, etc. If your mind isn't stable, you may lose focus and keep thinking about negative things. Fill your mind with positivity and knowledge; this will help you let go of the past and focus on the future. Moreover, 'knowledge is power.'

the more you learn and grow, the more power you will have over your emotional balance.

4. Divert Your Focus

One big mistake is thinking you can control how people act and think. Most of the time, your actions result from the decisions you make. You should know that you have the power to turn a negative experience into a positive one. The only thing you need to do is shift your focus away from negativity, events, and people beyond your control. You can't undo a split up from an unhealthy relationship, but you can learn from it. Remember, your past is not your future, and dwelling on the hurtful emotions will prevent you from experiencing an extraordinary life.

5. Focus on Personal Growth

Once you decide to let go, the next step is to work on your personal growth. Take time to figure out what you want to do with your life. It will help you divert attention from negative thoughts while simultaneously empowering you. Once you figure out what you wish to do, start working on achieving your goals. You can also partner with a career or personal coach to guide you during this stage.

Sometimes when we know the underlying cause, it is easier to manage our anger by refocusing our energy. I believe you understand that now, so let's practice this before moving on to the following technique.

Exercise #1

Maybe It's Not My Anger. Maybe It's...

Take a moment to think about how you feel when you are angry. Then pick one of the four emotions I covered in this chapter to focus on. Once you determine which emotion is at play;

1. Write about the event(s) that lead you to feel this way.

✎...

✎...

✎...

2. How will you deal with these emotions going forward?

✎...

✎...

✎...

7

#5 CHANGE YOUR FOCUS

"The best way to deal with anger is this: Acknowledge the presence of anger in your being and then consciously shift your focus from angry thoughts to empowering and uplifting thoughts."

— MUKESH

S ometimes when we are in the middle of our anger, it is hard to see a way out. The good news, though, is that it is not impossible. Now that you know that anger is a normal emotion and you can figure out your anger triggers, the next thing to do is to change your focus. Changing focus is personal; it cannot be replicated by someone else.

When you change your focus, you view life and its issues differently. You realize that dwelling too much on anger only wears you down. Although there are several things to do to adjust focus, pick one that best works for you. Although the process might require trial and error, do not give up when one process fails. It will help if you consistently practice until you achieve your goal.

With that said, I will be discussing five effective ways to change your focus. I will give detailed explanations, including step-by-step guides on how best to direct your focus away from anger. And as in previous chapters, there will be an exercise at the end of the chapter to help you get the best out of this anger management strategy.

REFRAME YOUR THINKING

Reframing is a method used in Cognitive Behavioral Therapy (CBT) to spot automatic thoughts and substitute them with more organized thoughts. I will explain CBT extensively in the next chapter. However, reframing your thinking is essential for discovering and stopping negative thoughts/distortions. Reframing is vital for breaking the stress cycle, depression, and anxiety. You can be free from negative thinking by simply reframing your thoughts. Negative thinking can hold you down from achieving great things in life. For example, Jake had a negative view of relationships, making him lose his connections with others whom he desired a lasting connection with. The following techniques helped him get back on track, and I believe they can help you too:

Note Your Thoughts

To reframe your thoughts, you must first understand what you are thinking. Being aware is a crucial first step in reframing. Whenever you sense a powerful emotion, such as anxiety deep down inside, stop and ask yourself, "What am I thinking right now?' I would advise you to write down your answer. This will give you something tangible to work with when it's time to reframe. At the same time, you'll also have a record of the kind of thought patterns you're prone to. Hiding a thought rather than facing it head-on might make you feel more worried, so admitting it is beneficial. Acknowledging your thoughts by writing them down reduces stress, anxiety, and ultimately anger.

Begin Fact-Checking Yourself

Many cognitive distortions lead us to believe things that aren't true in the first place. Make it a practice to ask yourself, "What proof do I have for this thought?" Asking this will improve your ability to recognize and rapidly shut down the lies your fear tells you. Perhaps you're thinking, "I need to go to the grocery store, but I'll become sick if I go." It is always disturbing when you assume the worst-case situation will occur. Ask yourself, "Okay, what proof do I have that I'll surely get sick if I go to the store?"

You need to question your thinking at this point. You are doing this to reframe your thoughts. By reframing the situation, you are separating emotional ideas from objective facts. As a result, you may remind yourself of the safety measures in place, such as stores restricting the number of people permitted inside at a time. There are also preventive measures available for you, like using hand sanitizer as you leave the store and washing your hands as soon as you get home.

Jake's thoughts were usually in the range of "this person will hurt me if I relate with them." However, he tried to channel his thoughts to remember his friend who had his back against bullies. He began to accept that he could do better with relationships and that constructive and robust lasting relationships were possible.

Be Realistic

When people hear "reframe your thoughts," they often assume it means turning a negative concept into something lovely. However, the opposite of an unhelpful thought is a realistic notion, not a positive one. For instance, let's say you have no symptoms or cause to assume you have coronavirus. However, you are plagued with thoughts that coronavirus would kill you. A reframed thought won't necessarily translate to you never catching coronavirus and being perfectly fine.

Instead, it would mean that you may not be sick and have a minimal risk of contracting the disease because you have chosen to isolate yourself socially. It is also useful when attempting to foresee an uncertain future, rather than only the risk of what may become. Yes, many things may not be going well in the world. Many of these things are beyond your control, and there is little or nothing you can do to change them. Remember that our attitude determines a great deal of our response, and dwelling on problems or past events will not serve you in any productive way.

Think About the Reply You Would Give A Friend with The Same Thoughts

We are, on average, kinder to the people we care about than we are to ourselves. Consider the last time you indulged in some destructive self-talk and said or thought things about yourself that you would never think of (much less speak to) a friend. Similarly, thinking about how you'd comfort a friend engaged in an anxious thought loop can help you be more compassionate to yourself.

Mentally Escape

Not everybody has the luxury of getting on the next flight for an island getaway. Anger can be so draining, and you will agree that it is not so easy to cope with it. Therefore, you may need to escape from reality once in a while. However, there are other simple steps to help you escape mentally. Doing this will take some practice, but it is a great way to handle whatever life throws. Here, I'll be discussing three powerful strategies to help you escape mentally.

1. Clearing Your Mind

▷ Meditate

Meditation is a great way to clear your mind. It is used traditionally to transition the mind to a place of calmness. The exciting aspect is that you can do it in the comfort of your home, and it does not require any expertise. All you need to do is look for a calm environment without distractions. Your environment should also be quiet and at a comfortable temperature.

There is no "appropriate" position for meditation. Choose a position that feels perfect for you. Some people prefer to lie or sit on the ground, while others prefer a meditation bench. Just ensure you are comfortable and able to relax completely. Once comfortable, close your eyes. Closing your eyes helps you avoid distractions by tuning out other things around you. Sometimes, it may be helpful to cover your eyes with a towel or a mask. You can also use earplugs if your environment makes it challenging to tune out distractions.

During meditation, remain conscious of your breathing. You don't necessarily need to control it. Just breathe naturally and be aware of your breath. With practice, you will be able to clear your mind during meditation and will find yourself feeling calm and relaxed.

▷ Listen to Music

Another fantastic way to clear your mind is to listen to music. Moreover, they say, "music is life." It is an important way of clearing your mind. Scientific findings show that music has various positive effects on the different areas of the brain. Thus, it assists with regulating your mood and improving your self-awareness. If you do not know the genre of music you prefer, you can listen to binaural beats. Classical music like Piano Concertos is a great option as well. If you desire something more lively, you can try some drum and bass music without lyrics.

▷ Practice Yoga

Yoga helps you focus on your mind and body. It allows you to escape reality while simultaneously having a physical workout. Aside from the physical health benefits of yoga, there are many psychological and mental benefits. Recent studies have found that yoga can help reduce stress, relieve anxiety and depression, and improve social attachments. These days, you will find therapists including yoga as a complementary form of psychotherapy. It is an excellent tool outside the therapy office to cope with stress and anxiety and heal emotional wounds.

Sometimes, working through your body is just what you need to escape reality and get moving. Signing up for a yoga class is a way to rid your mind of several mental impurities and decrease anger triggers. The focus moves inward to tranquility, peace, and calmness in a yoga class.

2. Using Activities To Escape Mentally

▷ Spend Time Alone

Your spouse, children, and co-workers are probably a part of your daily life. Escaping mentally means temporarily leaving them behind to refocus on yourself. You may need to turn off your phone to eliminate social media and other distractions. Temporarily disconnecting from everything and everyone allows us to slow the pace of our thoughts and focus inward. I suggest waking up about 30 minutes or one hour before everyone else to enjoy and appreciate the morning's beauty fully. First thing in the morning is also an excellent time for meditation and reflection.

The world we live in is filled with several stressors. Therefore, having some dedicated time to yourself can help refresh your mind, giving you the chance to handle things more adequately whenever you return. In short, solitude helps your brain "reboot."

▷ *Read a Book*

Books are ideal for mental escape as they allow your thoughts to enter another realm. This is an enjoyable pastime for many and allows for physical relaxation while also providing a temporary mental break. I recommend you read a book that throws you into the world of "make-believe." you can pick a book from your favorite collections, a best-seller, a time-honored classic, or a book with a title that interests you. Works of historical fiction such as Lord of the Rings, Harry Potter, etc., are a perfect choice. If you want longer escapism, you can choose a series (a book available in a trilogy or more).

▷ *Try a Repetitive Activity*

Everyone is different. While some people find it more beneficial to engage in relatively dormant activities, others find calm, repetitive physical activities more helpful. These activities involve repetitive motions that distance your mind from reality and help you find solace. Knitting and painting are two examples of repetitive activities.

Going for a walk is another great activity for mental rest as it also offers physical advantages. Walking an average of 7000 steps daily is excellent for your health, and you can use that walking time to reflect and daydream. Some people may enjoy outdoor activities like hiking and fishing as they involve nature and add a bit of fun. The truth is, there is no "best" choice of activity for escaping mentally. The best thing is always to do something you enjoy.

▷ *Take Yourself on a Mini Retreat*

Pick a location you love; it could be anywhere you want. Select a specific time, one that is convenient for you. Take your journal along and take some time to write down your fears. Think about the many things that bother you, things that may be delaying your journey towards anger management. Write those things down and then physically burn them, showing that you no longer want to carry the burden. Make space for a new reality by writing down the things you wish to let in. Manifest your desired change and make it clear to yourself.

You can also drive, try a new wine, see a movie or visit a museum. Ensure you do something that you do not do regularly. Going to a new place helps you escape the real world. Sit back and appreciate the beauty around you. Think about the positive things in your life. Take a walk, enjoy the breeze, and smell the roses. Just do all the things you can to make yourself happy.

▷ Find Your Gratitude

Many of us experience gratitude daily, even if we aren't aware of it. By definition, gratitude means being "appreciative of benefits received" or "affording pleasure or contentment." Even simple acts like appreciating pleasant weather or loving the first taste of a delicious meal can elicit gratitude, thanks, or appreciation. However, it would help if you believed that appreciation is more than a feeling; it is also a strategy for reducing negative emotions.

During a recent reread of Viktor Frankl's "Man's Search For Meaning." He describes a "young woman whose death (he) observed in a concentration camp" in the book. He stated that the young woman "knew she would die in the following few days" and "despite this knowledge, she remained cheerful." Frankl explained that she chose "gratitude" over bitterness or rage as the basis of her joy.

This realization shifted my perspective on gratitude, turning it from a passive feeling to an action verb. If the woman in this narrative, who had already lost nearly everything dear to her, could choose gratitude over anger and resentment, why couldn't I? This realization inspired many other readers and me to make deliberate decisions to replace natural, reactionary sentiments with gratitude. I believe it can help you too!

▷ Practice Empathy

Empathy is when you feel people's hearts, listen to others, and see with other people's eyes. Empathy is so important in your daily life. Lack of empathy causes poor communication and a failure to understand others. Divorce, breakups, war, and kidnapping are results of a lack of empathy. Although you cannot control how others think, you certainly can control your thoughts. Three essential skills are required to moderate our anger with enhanced empathy: listening, self-awareness, and acceptance.

Empathic listening is a style that goes above and beyond simply hearing what someone has to say.

Empathetic listening is a form of listening that uses another person's point of view to experience the world through their eyes. It gives you a better grasp of how others are feeling. As you gain a deeper understanding of your ideas and feelings, you develop self-awareness. You'll understand someone else's ideas and feelings more effectively. The more open you are to others' sentiments, the better you are at reading others' feelings and the less enraged you become toward them.

Acceptance, on another note, is the ability to notice that others have a right to their "bizarre" emotions. Others' feelings are beyond your control. You must enable people to communicate their feelings without dictating how they should feel. Empathic people realize how tough it is to regulate one's emotions. Accepting others means that we recognize that they are doing their best, given the circumstances. Remember, if they thought they could do better, they would.

Accepting others' feelings can be a little challenging when they behave differently than we do. We all struggle with those who have different characters from us. We will be best equipped to understand ourselves and others if we master the art of empathy.

Here are five straightforward guidelines to help you become more empathic.

1. Pay attention to how others express their emotions. Keep your eyes peeled for both verbal and nonverbal cues. Make an effort to decipher the message hidden within the words and actions.
2. Put other people's feelings ahead of your own. Allow yourself to put your demands and ideas aside long enough to hear what someone else says.
3. Explain what you learned to demonstrate that you understand the messages you receive or respond to.
4. Avoid interruptions. Allow speakers to finish their sentences before speaking.
5. Inquire about additional information. If you still don't understand, keep asking questions until you do.

▷ Channel Your Energy Into a New Hobby

Learning a new skill, being outdoors, reading, or doing something musical are fantastic ways to spend your free time and avoid your usual stressful routine. Spending time doing something you enjoy benefits your mental health and well-being. According to research, people who have hobbies are less prone to experience stress, low mood, or sadness. Get-out-and-about activities can make you feel happier and calmer.

Group activities, such as team sports, can help you further develop communication skills and enhanced interpersonal interactions.

Your passions may be artistic, athletic, scholarly, or entirely different. You can pick a hobby that you can do alone or with others. Whatever your desires are, there will be a pastime for you out there. It doesn't matter what it is as long as it is relevant and pleasurable to you. Doing something out of passion rather than obligation is soothing. Even a modest amount of time spent doing something you enjoy can help balance out the stressors of everyday life.

Now that you understand how to change your focus for increased emotional control take the exercise below to evaluate what you will be changing.

<u>Exercise</u>

What Can I Do?

1. How do you think you can reframe your thinking to manage your anger?

✎...

✎...

✎...

2. What are the various ways you can mentally escape?

✎...

✎...

✎...

3. Do you feel the need to be full of gratitude rather than resentment?

✎...

✎...

✎...

4. How can you be more empathetic?

✎...

✎...

✎...

5. What hobby will you be focusing your energy on?

✎...

✎...

✎...

8

#6 EMPLOY CBT STRATEGIES

"The problem is not the problem. The problem is your attitude about the problem."

— PIRATES OF THE CARIBBEAN

---

nger is not restricted to yelling and shouting. The outcomes of anger vary from person to person. Some people hurt themselves, while others feel bad about their anger, leading to feelings of guilt. Your attitude towards your anger plays a significant role in managing your anger. In the previous chapter, you learned how to control your anger by changing your focus.

In addition to shifting focus, another effective technique for anger control is cognitive-behavioral therapy (CBT). The effects of CBT are fascinating and can be one of the most powerful tools available to you. I will expand on this technique and teach you how to use it. This chapter will also cover other therapies for anger management and how you can get the best out of them.

WHAT IS COGNITIVE BEHAVIORAL THERAPY

Cognitive-behavioral therapy (CBT) is a psychological treatment effective for various problems such as anxiety disorders, depression, mental disorders, marital problems, and many more. This therapy often proves more effective than many other psychiatric medications or psychological therapy. A lot of research demonstrates that CBT improves the quality and functioning of life. It works on three core principles, which are:

1. Psychological issues are based, in part, on meaningless, faulty ways of thinking.
2. Psychological issues are based, in part, on learned patterns of useless behavior.
3. People who suffer from psychological problems can learn the best ways of managing them,

thereby reducing their symptoms and boosting the quality of their lives.

CBT strategies involve changing your behavioral patterns. These changes may include facing your fears rather than avoiding them. It may also mean using the role-playing technique to prepare yourself for potential problematic interactions. You also learn to relax your body and calm your mind.

CBT allows you to be your therapist. With constant practice, you will learn various coping mechanisms. You can also learn to change the way you reason, thus changing your behavior and problematic emotions. CBT helps analyze what is going on in your life instead of focusing solely on the problems. The primary aim is to look for ways to move forward in time by developing coping mechanisms to deal with your anger.

HOW CBT CAN HELP MANAGE ANGER

Do you get annoyed when someone tells you to control your anger, especially when you do not even know how to go about it? I'm sure you wonder how belief systems are related to anger management. CBT for anger management might sound extreme or drastic, but it is tamer than you think. Your belief system is your value, expectation, needs, perception of life, and personality. However, these beliefs change with time and pertain to every aspect of your life. Belief systems deal with thoughts and emotions. Therefore, constantly falling back on such views can cause an increase in negative thinking and emotions.

A consistent negative belief can lead to severe anxiety, depression, anger, guilt, and chronic stress. Your reactions to a situation are based on your belief system and experiences. An event that occurred in the past, and your belief about that event, will influence your reaction and perception of the event. For instance, Jake was bullied (the situation), and he believes his voice won't change anything (the belief), so he continues to get bullied (the outcome).

Changing your belief system can be difficult, but it is achievable. CBT will help you recognize your belief system. Then you can discuss and analyze the beliefs. After analyzing your belief system, you can design a new belief system by thinking, journaling, or doing mindfulness exercises. CBT incorporates mindfulness techniques like meditation or breathing techniques for at least twenty minutes a day. Doing these will help you get a hold of your anger and emotion.

Anger is unpredictable. It can pop up anytime, even when you least expect it. Most people have said hurtful words due to anger during a conversation, which has caused resentment or embarrassment. CBT strategies can help control anger during conversations by teaching you not to think that the other person intended to make you angry. It teaches you not to focus on the person but on the stressor. You will also learn to use 'I' to communicate your emotions with this strategy.

USING CBT TO COMBAT ANGER

Cognitive therapy (CBT) is not just one therapy but a combination of effective therapies that work in conjunction to effectively control unhealthy emotions. The following CBT techniques are effective in combating anger.

Accept your Anger and Retrieve Your Emotional Balance

The first step toward proper anger control is accepting your anger and retrieving your emotional balance. Doing this will help you focus more on the healing details you will discover as you get more information about your anger. You have now begun to identify your anger cues. These cues can be mental, emotional, or physical. Cognitive signals include distorted thinking and using terms like definitely, always, must, etc. Examples of physical cues are tight muscles, clenched fists, upset stomach, and headaches.

Try to recognize your cues. With time, you'll know what works best for you and what feels right. After identifying your anger cues, the next step is to retrieve your emotional balance. This can be achieved by diaphragmatic breathing to increase the oxygen level in your body system. Practicing this step can be as simple as the following:

1. Lie down on your back and place your hand on your stomach
2. Observe the way your stomach is rising
3. Inhale down to your abdomen and observe your hand rising as the belly expands and contracts.

Mindful breathing, such as the one I described above, will help you reduce anxiety, prevent burnout, and decrease negative emotions. The purpose of this breathing exercise is to anchor yourself in the present. Once completed, you will worry less about the past or the future.

Expressing yourself by talking the situation out is another helpful strategy for regaining emotional balance. It prevents you from bottling the anger inside you while informing the other person of your displeasure. You can also write a letter to yourself or the person you feel directly contributed to the situation. In doing this, write without pause or any self-judgment or criticism. Write until the emotions dissipate and all hostility has been transferred to paper. You can then burn, trash, or even choose to share this letter with the person or someone else you trust.

Take Note of Your Feelings and Thoughts

There is a well-known link between your feelings and behaviors; they have significant impacts on one another. But where do your thoughts fit into all of this? Whenever we mention 'thoughts,' we refer to different mental activities such as hopes, wishes, predictions, plans, memories, and judgments. One effective way of tackling anger issues is by changing key behaviors, one of the most direct CBT strategies.

Generally, people often don't notice their thoughts. These thoughts are usually pushed to the background, assisting with automatic decision-making and task completion. Experts also discovered that automatic thoughts directly and immediately impact emotions, feelings, and ultimately behaviors. To better understand this, try to imagine this scenario:

Imagine walking home alone one dark evening, wondering about what to eat for dinner. Suddenly, you hear a rustling noise towards your left. What is it?

Thought 1: "It is a cat."

What is the effect of this thought on your emotions? How do you react? You probably think to yourself, "ok, it's just a cat. I can stay calm and keep walking home. Maybe I will have a steak and salad for dinner."

Thought 2: "It's a mugger."

What is the effect of this thought on your emotions? How do you react? This thought will probably make you feel something different. You may begin to feel tense, fearful, or anxious. You may also feel some sensations in your body such as sweaty palms, increased heart rate, churning stomach, etc. What do you do at this point? You perhaps walk faster or find somewhere to hide. Suddenly, a cat walks out from the trash can behind the wall. You then take a deep breath and begin the mental and physical process of relaxing back into "normal."

This simple illustration shows that only a thought (not fact) can change how you feel and what you do. Therefore, taking note of your cognitions (thoughts and feelings) and your behavior is an excellent way of understanding your emotions. This is the foundation of Cognitive Behavioral Therapy (CBT).

Pay attention to how you react to different situations. Think about what triggered you. Take note of your feelings and thoughts after the whole situation. You can also write your thoughts and feelings in a journal. Jake did this, and it helped him understand his emotions better, calmed his mind, and gave him a private space for himself. He became more at peace with himself, felt at ease, and related better with other people.

Know Your Worth and Potentials

There are so many "self-" words out there. They include self-esteem, self-respect, self-love, self-confidence, self-acceptance, etc. These words describe how you feel, think, and act towards yourself. One "self" word that is at the core of everything you do (your thoughts, feelings, and behaviors) is self-worth. It describes how you view your value and worthiness as a human being. While it may be quite tricky to improve self-worth in adults, it is not impossible.

The first thing you need to do is look back at the various things that do not determine self-worth. Your attractiveness, job title, social media following, bank account, etc., do not specify how worthy or valuable you are as a person. The world we are in today may distract you from chasing status, popularity, and money. I encourage you to pause, take a step back and think about what truly matters in self-worth. These things include compassion, empathy, kindness, respect for other people, and how well you treat people around you.

After this, you can now work on identifying your critical inner voice. This inner critic is always trying to nitpick your flaws and point them out. People often let this inner critic get the best of them, but if you let it win too often, the critic may start thinking that it is correct. Whenever you begin to notice this inner critic firing up, pause and ask yourself if there is any basis for the criticism. If none of it makes sense to you, feel free to shut out this inner critic. Remember that you are worthy and valuable, regardless of what you do.

Once you understand, love, and accept yourself, you will get to a point where you don't have to depend on external factors for self-worth. The best thing to do at this point is to recognize your self-worth and appreciate yourself. However, you must also remember to maintain self-understanding, self-love, and self-acceptance. You have enough power to respond to circumstances and events based on internal resources at this stage. These resources are the true reflection of your value.

Identify Your Unfulfilled Needs

You are likely aware when you start feeling frustrated, resentful, or angry. However, most people don't pause to ask, "What exactly do I need right now?" You will often find out that the answer to this question is not what you think. You think you are angry at your kids for cluttering the room with their shoes when in reality, it is their cooperation you need. Their collaboration allows you to work together and feel more connected to them. On the other hand, it may mean that you need more order to contribute to a sense of peace. These are two different needs.

Many times we get angry; some of our top emotional needs include:

- **Love and Connection** - a sense of belonging, acceptance, and support.
- **Certainty** - a sense of safety, security, and comfort.
- **Significance** - a sense of individuality, uniqueness, and being special.
- **Growth** - a desire to learn and evolve.
- **Variety** - a sense of adventure, interest, and change.
- **Contribution** - the willingness to give to the people around us.

You want your emotions to inform you, not rule you. Therefore, awareness is critical! You need to slow down and notice how your distressing feelings are arising. Simply do the following:

STOP

PAUSE

TAKE A BREATH

Then ask yourself: why do I really want or need it right now?

Getting an answer to this question will help you better communicate the problem and find the solution. It will also help you respond better when angry.

Take Action to Meet Your Need

The great thing about understanding your needs is that you can begin to take responsibility for meeting those needs. Let's take Jake's case, for example, again. The question on his mind was, "how can I increase the feeling of being supported?" He said to his friend, "I need support. I am drifting away, being more alone since my girlfriend left me. What can you help me with so that I won't be alone in this world?"

If your unmet need is respect, you can join a volunteer team where you take up a leadership role and earn respect from other members. Essentially, identify your meet, formulate a plan to meet that need, and take action! Furthermore, these new insights will help you interpret and react to situations more constructively. Change like this often takes some time and patience. Do not get discouraged if you don't see immediate results. Remember to feel good about progress, bit or small, and know that you are doing your part in moving the needle forward.

Let Go of Your Fears

Excessive fear and worry are often troubling emotions that tie into anger. One powerful CBT technique for conquering your fears is evaluation. During this technique, you evaluate the fear to determine if it is productive or unproductive and learn how to let go of useless fears. Answers to the following questions can help you determine if your fear is aiding in your progression or hindering progress.

I. **What is your prediction, and how likely will it happen?** You must identify this in detail. For example, you can be scared that people will laugh at you while giving a speech. You may be scared of being fired if you make mistakes at work. Whatever the situation, state the leading cause of your fear precisely. Once you know this, create evidence-based predictions on how likely it will occur. How many times has such a thing happened?

Are there steps you can take to prevent such fear from coming true? How can you possibly influence the outcome of the situation?

II. **What are the most likely scenarios and the best-case scenario?** Instead of focusing on the worst possibility, you should also consider the best case. Your mind will likely drift towards the extreme potentials, but they happen less often in reality. Think of other possible scenarios. For instance, "I will give the speech; there will be some truly engaged listeners and others who may be bored."

III. **How many times has your prediction come true?** You can also evaluate the usefulness of your fear by counting the number of times the worst thing happened. For example, suppose you've driven on the freeway 50 times in the past three months and never had an accident. In that case, odds indicate your fear is disproportionate.

IV. **If the worst case happens, how will you cope?** Most people tend to end their ominous predictions in the worst situations. It is best to think about your following action; what you will do if there is a problematic situation.

V. **What are the benefits and costs of the fear?** Finally, ask yourself if it is worth it to be fearful about the situation. While some degree of fear may motivate you towards preparing for the outcomes, too much fear may cause you to lose focus. You may not have control over things, and it's helpful to realize that. Whenever you identify your fear as unproductive, tell yourself that thinking about it is of no use now. Let it go! After this, refocus your mind immediately on crucial matters. The more you learn to let go of your worries, the less consuming power you give them.

Look at Things from the Other Person's Perspective

The moment you notice a positive change in your self-esteem, you are ready for this step. Here, you analyze the other person's point of view. It involves the evaluation of the other person's unmet needs and what triggered them to act the way they did. People also have their own unmet needs and their ways of satisfying them. Until you genuinely make an effort, you may not understand the other person. You will keep seeing the person as an enemy because you have created an opinion about them, causing you to be less objective and narrowing your perception.

However, you need to take your blinders off and widen your horizon. Make room for other people and their shortcomings. This technique does not only help you dissipate your anger. It also empowers you towards creating your goal and seeing people fully. When you try to understand that a person may be emotionally disturbed by some events in their lives, you will begin to show empathy and sensitivity. Ask yourself, "why did she act defensively?" "Could she be angry about something in her life?" Answering these questions will significantly value allowing you to look outside of yourself and your emotional interpretations.

Learn to Forgive

Forgiveness is an act you practice to heal yourself from unhealthy situations. It helps you move on and set you free from the captivity of past events. Forgiveness occurs in three phases. They are:

1. Accepting the reality
2. Recognizing the growth and healing you have achieved
3. Wishing for growth and healing for the other person

Wishing other people growth and success is an act of compassion. Doing this will disconnect you from the hurtful situation. It also helps you see yourself as a powerful and balanced person. Recognizing the frame of reference of the other person will spur you to wish them growth and healing as you would want for your-self. You have an increased sense of contentment and happiness, and you can move forward and continue development.

THERAPY FOR ANGER MANAGEMENT

Besides cognitive behavioral therapy, several other treatments can help with your anger management journey. These therapies aim to minimize anger-evoking and stressful situations. They also help you improve your self-control and healthily express your feelings.

Other Therapies for Anger Management

Besides CBT, there are other effective therapies for anger management. In this section, I will discuss three of the most effective ones.

▷ *Psychodynamic Therapy*

Psychodynamic therapy is a technique that facilitates a deeper understanding of your emotions and several other mental processes. This therapy aims at helping you examine the psychological causes of your anger and how you respond to it. It enables you to gain more significant insights into how you think and feel. Improving your understanding will help you make better choices about your life, improve your relationships, and work towards satisfaction and happiness.

Generally, this therapy involves talking to a professional about the problems you face with the belief that you will find solutions. Working with a psychodynamic therapist will help you better understand your feelings, thoughts, and other emotions that contribute to your behaviors. Furthermore, it will help you identify some unconscious causes of your feelings and actions. Psychodynamic therapy is an effective anger management therapy. It promotes insight, self-regulation, and emotional growth. Some of the essential aspects of this therapy are:

I. **Identifying Patterns.** Here, you can recognize the different patterns in relationships and behaviors. Many people have distinctive ways of responding to issues without understanding the tendencies. However, psychodynamic therapy will teach you how to spot them and the best approaches to coping with situations.

II. **Understanding Emotions.** With good insights, you can recognize patterns contributing to emotional dysfunction. Thus, making changes becomes easy. This therapy is also helpful for understanding and exploring emotions.

III. **Improving Relationships.** One other primary focus of psychodynamic therapy is relationships with other people. As you work with a therapist, you better understand how you respond to other people. Doing this will help you improve your responses and develop healthier relationships.

▷ *Dialectical Behavioral Therapy (DBT)*

This therapy aims to teach you how to live in the moment, regulate your emotions, cope with stress, and improve your relationship with other people. DBT is a modified type of CBT that can help people with chronic anger and emotional issues. It works by developing distress tolerance skills and emotional regulation, effective communication in relationships, and mindfulness. Some of the strategies used in DBT are:

I. **Core Mindfulness.** As we established in chapter 5, mindfulness is an essential anger management technique. One of the crucial benefits of DBT is that it helps you develop mindfulness skills. Being mindful keeps you focused on present moments. Therefore, you pay more attention to your feelings, thoughts, impulses, and sensations. It also helps you use your senses to understand the happenings around you without being judgemental. The technique also creates calmness and prevents you from engaging in negative thoughts and impulsive behaviors. Any of the mindfulness skills discussed in chapter 5 will be effective here.

II. **Distress Tolerance.** This DBT strategy helps you accept your current situation. It teaches you to handle situations using techniques like distractions, self-soothing treatments, improving the moment, etc. This strategy also prepares you for intense emotions while empowering you to cope with those emotions with a positive long-term outlook. A sample exercise would be to put your body in charge. How? If you are inside when you start getting the feelings of anger, go outside. Get up and gently run up and down the stairs if you are lying down. The idea is to create a distraction, doing other activities that will take your mind off the feeling.

III. **Interpersonal Effectiveness.** This technique is your best choice if you want to be more assertive in your relationships without being rude or hostile. It teaches you proper listening and communicative processes, how to deal with difficult people, and how to respect yourself. One simple exercise I use in this case is GIVE:

Gentle – Don't threaten, judge, or attack others.
Interest – Show interest using good listening
skills. Never interrupt someone while speaking.
Validate – Acknowledge other people's feelings
and thoughts.
Easy – Smile often, stay light-hearted, and enjoy
your relationship with others.

IV. **Emotion Regulation**. Here, you are taught to use your powerful feelings positively and effectively. What you learn in this case will allow you to recognize and cope with intense emotions like anger. For example, suppose you feel angry and do not want to see your family and friends. In this case, make plans to meet and spend time with your loved ones. That is, you identify your feeling and do the exact opposite. Anger often comes with intense feelings of displeasure and the urge to react negatively. Recognizing these feelings and labeling them as "negative" or "unproductive" will help you channel your energy towards the opposite— "positive" and "productive." Doing this will reduce your emotional vulnerability and give you more positive experiences.

▷ *Family Therapy*

This type of therapy is effective when the anger is aimed toward family members. Family therapy can help you resolve issues and boost communication within the family unit. It also enables you to understand the different people in your family better, thus allowing relationships to flourish and grow. Family therapy sessions will teach you the best ways to own your emotions and prevent yourself from hurting your loved ones. It will help you develop strategies like:

i. How to regulate your emotions
ii. How to manage conflicts productively
iii. Ways of being a more understanding partner
iv. How to bring up your children without affecting their developing minds with your unresolved issues.

While the above therapies may involve meeting with a professional, the final anger management technique we will discuss in our next chapter is pretty straightforward – creating a Cool Down Kit. Before we go any further, please take some time to complete the following exercise.

Exercise

Who/What is Responsible?

Think back to a time when you felt angry and guilty at the same time. (Example: Last month, I tripped and knocked our television over, shattering it.)

i. What was your initial belief? State how strong it is in percentage.

(Example: I was to blame for the television that broke (99%))

✎...

ii. Identify all the different factors involved in the situation. Weight these factors in terms of percentage.

Example:

- My brother was blocking my view (10%)
- He did not answer me when I told him to leave (10%)

✎...

✎...

✎...

iii. Get a revised belief and percentage rating to reflect an overall picture. While doing this, consider the factors you can control and those you have no control over. This will help you get a good view of the situation and a reflective percentage rating.

Example: I can control what happens in my house better (80%)

✎...

✎...

✎...

#7 CREATE A COOL DOWN KIT

"Calmness is the cradle of power."

— JOSIAH GILBERT HOLLAND

Regulating emotions is one of the most complex tasks for anyone. According to the quote above, you cannot possess power without calmness. We face several stressful conditions regularly, be it finances, relationships, work, or health. Responses to the stress often wear down the body, draining your energy and affecting your health. Stress also affects your decision-making and the way you manage your emotions. When tightly wound up, you will most likely react poorly to situations instead of responding with reason. Furthermore, a stressed mind makes you narrowly focused, preventing you from viewing the world from a broader perspective. This often leads to clouded judgments and inappropriate behaviors.

However, your attention becomes broader when you're calm; you see the bigger picture of different situations. Having a relaxed, rested mind does not mean you'll drown under your responsibilities. Instead, it will bring you enhanced attention, greater energy, and the needed creativity to handle different emotions. You will have the ability to manage your energy in stressful situations so that you won't constantly be burning yourself up. Calmness keeps you focused on the right things to do and how best to get them done.

If you've been finding it hard to create a cool-down kit, this chapter will break it down and provide you with a list of possible items to include in your kit. Depending on your needs and preferences, you can add many things to your cool-down kit. Therefore, I find this final anger management technique very effective as it is the most creative way of managing your anger.

WHAT IS A COOL DOWN KIT, AND WHAT IS IT USED FOR?

A cool-down kit is a box that contains everything you need to control your emotions. It includes things you can feel with your five senses (sight, touch, smell, hearing, and taste). As the name implies, a cool-down kit has various things to keep you calm in difficult situations, especially when you are angry. This kit should be created according to your interests, although I recommend including some general items.

A cool-down kit is an excellent idea for developing emotional control. It fuels self-soothing behaviors by fostering self-awareness. When you understand yourself and your feelings, you will be able to control impulsive behavior effectively. You'll also focus on the beneficial responses.

A cool-down kit is excellent for your attention and concentration. Depending on what you have in your kit, you can massively improve your focus while assisting you to express your feelings in the safest possible ways. At the same time, you become more aware of your triggers, feelings, and problem-solving processes. The items in your kit will help you quickly identify and differentiate internal signals and filter the effective from the destructive.

Jake created his cool-down kit, and it worked like a charm. He added things he loves and a few other general things. Two items were particularly essential in his kit — his journal and headphones. Jake had developed an attachment to classical music, making it feel exceptionally natural for him to tune into this coping mechanism when the need arose. At the same time, he would bring out his journal, where he would write how he was feeling at that time. These activities distracted him from the anger triggers, providing better control over his emotions.

HOW TO CREATE YOUR COOL DOWN KIT

It's pretty simple! Get a small to a medium-sized box or something similar that can safely hold the items you would like to put in your kit. Then, include things that help you become more aware of yourself and your environment. These items should aid adequate and healthy expression of your feelings while allowing you to stay calm.

Your five senses offer the most effective assistance when deciding what to put in your kit:

Sight-Pictures of the people you love, your writings of inspirational words, a journal, clear scenery images, etc.

Touch – Stress ball, a piece of jewelry, puzzle games, playing cards, prayer beads, etc.

Smell – Lotions, candles, fragrances, essential oils, etc.

Hearing – Uplifting songs, sounds of nature (wind blowing leaves, running water, chime balls, etc.)

Taste – Favorite mint, gum, or candy.

WHAT SHOULD YOU PUT IN YOUR COOL DOWN KIT?

Depending on the five sense organs, you can put many things in a cool-down kit. You do not necessarily have to include everything I will mention below. You can select a few things you relate to and some other general items. You can even add other items that are not on the list.

- Fidgets – These small toys give tactile stimulation and are suitable for keeping hands busy!
- Weighted stuffed animals
- Small weighted blanket
- Theraputty
- Play-Doh
- Slime
- Bubble wrap

- Therapy brush – Great tools for sensory regulation and deep massage.
- Eye mask
- Massager
- Stress balls
- Pipe cleaners – For soft touch and fidgety hands
- Playing cards
- Find it games – These games are lovely! They typically have a lot of rice or beads inside with some tiny toys or shapes to look for. You can also make your own.
- Fabric scraps or scarves – For soft touch and fidgety hands
- Puzzles
- Question cards – You can purchase them or create your own
- Word searches
- Blank notepads
- Affirmation cards – You can create your own or purchase them
- Etch-A- Sketch
- Coloring books
- Brain quest cards
- Mini chalk and chalkboard
- Whistle
- Headphones – Noise canceling work best

- Rubik's cube
- Audiobooks
- Crosswords
- Drawings
- Harmonica
- Spinning top
- Tissue paper for tearing
- Legos
- Balance cushion
- Small mirror
- Essential oils
- Yoga cards
- Scratch and sniff stickers
- Deep breathing printout
- Scented candles
- Emotion cards
- Hard candy
- Chewelry – Usually bracelets or necklaces designed for chewing.
- Chewing gum
- Jump ropes
- Gummy snacks
- Crunchy snacks
- Hand weights – No more than a couple of pounds
- Exercise ball
- Resistance bands

- Lava lamp
- Sunglasses
- Kaleidoscope
- Bubbles
- Snow globe
- Photo album
- Hourglass

Ensure that you set up your kit with items that cover the five senses so that it can serve its purpose. Whenever you feel angry, utilize these tools to change your sensory perception and response. Squeezing and stretching things may be a way you cope with stress, so you want to have your stress ball and stretchy strings handy. After creating your cool-down kit, you will want to ensure you have a designated spot for it, preferably a desirable location. It may be your bedroom, living room, or another place you often occupy.

Although this idea may sound juvenile, it has been well studied and proven effective for many adults. Give it a try, and you may be surprised how well you respond to having your customized kit.

You now have all of the tools to conquer your anger. Does this mean you will never be angry again? No. But does it mean you will be better able to manage your anger the next time it decides to show itself? Absolutely

Exercise

My Cool Down Kit

Write down at least ten items you will include in your cool-down kit, and how you feel each of the items will help you control your anger.

1.

2.

3.

4.

5.

6.

7.

8.

9.

10.

BONUS: JOURNAL PROMPTS

"Journal writing, when it becomes a ritual for trans-formation, is not only life-changing but life-expanding."

— JENNIFER WILLIAMSON

I n chapter 4, I briefly discussed the importance of journaling for anger management. Journaling, otherwise known as freewriting, can improve your mental health, physical health, and mood. This tool is relatively straightforward; you can make it your safe space. We focused on trigger journals as an excellent technique for general anger management.

Journaling is a great tool to get rid of negative thoughts and allow more positivity into your life. It helps create a world of calm when all we feel is chaos. Not sure how or where to start or the things to write? Use the prompts provided here to center yourself and regain control of your thoughts and emotions. Furthermore, I will provide you with 30 journal prompts to help you get started in this chapter!

WHY ARE JOURNAL PROMPTS IMPORTANT FOR ANGER MANAGEMENT?

Putting feelings of anger into writing can help reduce the impulse of the initial sensation and prevent the anger from escalating. Writing these feelings on paper often makes it easier to understand the underlying emotions behind the anger (such as sadness, guilt, jealousy, etc.). It also allows you to view the situation from a detached standpoint. You consider it as if you are an observer of the anger feelings and not the host. From this vantage point, you can process the emotions more appropriately.

30 JOURNAL PROMPTS FOR ANGER MANAGEMENT

The following journal prompts are divided into two categories, past and present. Depending upon the situation or emotion you are working through, you may be drawn to one or both of these categories at any given time.

Past

1. When was a time you were so upset that you broke or threw something? What triggered your anger? How did you feel about the situation?

2. What did a close friend do to you that made you angry? Was it totally off base, or could you understand why they might have done so? What was said?

3. Was there a day every little thing got you infuriated? How did you react? What were the things that bothered you?

4. Describe a time you became angry when someone did the opposite of what you told them. How did you react to the situation? What other feelings (besides anger) did you have?

5. How angry have you ever made another person? Did you notice any visible effect on the person? Did the

person yell at you? If so, do you feel you evoked that response?

6. What thing got you silently angry for a few minutes until you couldn't hold it anymore and had to bring it up to another person? How did you solve the issue?

7. When did someone get angry at you for not giving them what they wanted? What happened, and how did you deal with it?

8. Did you ever get so angry that you almost hurt someone? What did the person do to make you feel like that? How was the issue resolved?

9. When was the last time you used a swear word or yelled out loud? What happened? What was your feeling after the reaction?

10. Did you ever get angry about things outside of your control? What was the situation, and how did you react to it?

11. What did your parent(s) do that made you angry? How did things go down, and how were they handled?

12. Was there a time you damaged your relationship with someone because of your anger? Describe the encounter in detail.

13. When did someone make you angry by taking your things without asking? Was the object returned in the same condition? Describe the experience.

14. When did you overreact in a lousy situation with people around you looking your way as if something was wrong with you? Could you have handled the situation differently?

15. Do you remember when you got angry because you learned someone had lied to you? How close was the person to you? What was the result of your anger?

Present

16. Do you have anyone in your family that constantly does something to provoke your anger? Who is this person, and why does what they do bother you?

17. What thing do you deal with daily that often frustrates or gets you angry? How do you cope with it? Is there a way to eliminate this daily frustration?

18. Are there people that you would never want to make angry? What will you avoid doing or saying to keep peace with them?

19. Who is the most important person(s) in your life? What are the top three things the person/people do that get you angry? What are the top three things you do to make the person(s) angry?

20. Imagine that you can say anything without repercussions. Write everything that comes to your mind. What do you say? Who do you say it to? How do you feel after speaking/writing it?

21. Are there any objects that have bad memories attached to them? What are the reasons for these feelings? Would you destroy these items if you had the chance? Do you believe you can learn to cope with these items?

22. Do you go to sleep angry most of the time? What are the things that come to your mind right before you sleep? Can you deal with these issues during the day before sleeping?

23. Look around the environment where you are journaling. Check for things that get you angry. Describe these things and how they make you feel.

24. What are the top three things that keep haunting you from your past and make you angry whenever you think about them? Why do they make you mad? Do you think you or someone else is at fault?

25. Is there any unfair thing someone is making you do? Why do you think it is unjust? Who else do you think should be doing it? What other ways would you like things to go?

26. Do you feel angry when someone leaves your life? Did someone abandon you recently? How else do you wish things would be?

27. Are you angry as you are writing in this journal? Write down your reasons.

28. How do you think your anger affects the people around you? What changes do you see in these people? Do they often withdraw or become upset with you? How do their reactions make you feel? What are the things you want to change?

29. What characteristics of the current generation make you angry? What changes would you love to see?

30. Whenever you get angry, how do you calm down? List these coping methods and how they help you.

The fantastic thing about journaling is that you can never get it wrong. There's no judgment whatsoever in the world of journaling. You own your journal, and it is for you only to read. You never have to worry about anything going wrong or offending anyone else. Journaling can help with any emotion you may be feeling. Put your pen to paper whenever you feel an extreme emotion and need a quick way to center yourself.

JUST FOR YOU!

A FREE GIFT TO OUR READERS

9 ways to control emotional outbursts! Simply scan the QR code below or click on this link to request access to this free resource!

CONCLUSION

"Anybody can become angry – that is easy, but to be angry with the right person and to the right degree and at the right time and for the right purpose, and in the right way – that is not within everybody's power and is not easy."

— ARISTOTLE

Remember, anger is a normal emotion that cannot be eradicated. Life is filled with pain, loss, frustration, and the unpredictable actions of other people. Despite your efforts, events will happen that will get you angry; sometimes, this anger will be justifiable. While you can't change this, you can change how you let these things affect you. You can control your reactions and responses to these events and prevent them from causing lasting damage.

As I mentioned several times in this book, anger does not have the power to control you or take on a life of its own. It results from some primary emotions such as fear, hurt, sadness, guilt, betrayal, etc. If your anger has been a protection against dangers and oppression, trust yourself enough to utilize the healthier anger management strategies discussed in this book.

Examining your lifestyle and understanding the changes you need to make is the first step toward anger management. Next, follow up by identifying and managing your anger triggers. A great way of working your trigger responses is to practice mindfulness. We discussed six mindfulness exercises that will guide you in your progress.

Furthermore, you may have to change your focus and reframe your thinking; there is always a way out. Using cognitive-behavioral therapy (CBT) to combat anger will offer you a massive leap towards proper control of your anger. The final technique discussed in this book was the creation of a cool-down kit. Most people think these kits are only effective for kids, but they are also surprisingly effective for adults. I advise you to take the initiative and include some of the items I highlighted in your cool-down kit. I could not ignore the importance of journal prompts for anger management and included 30 sample prompts as a bonus anger management technique.

Countless people have found success using these anger management techniques. It doesn't mean you will never be angry again, but you can manage your anger more efficiently. I urge you to begin your journey today and gain control of your anger and life.

I hope you have enjoyed this content as much as I enjoyed putting it together for you. Revisit these techniques often and use this book as a continued source of information and tools. My goal will always be to help at least one person be able to separate themselves from the grip of anger and gain control of their life. I appreciate your time and wish you nothing but the best as you move forward.

If you find this book enlightening and helpful, please leave a review so that others struggling can also find the proper techniques to manage their anger.

Take care and remember... You are not alone!

REFERENCES

Baron, R. A. (1983). *The control of human aggression: An optimistic perspective.* Journal of Social and Clinical Psychology, 1, 97-119

Brad, J. B. (2002). *Does Venting Anger Feed or Extinguish the Flame? Catharsis, Rumination, Distraction, Anger, and Aggressive Responding.* Personality and Social Psychology Bulletin. doi.org/10.1177/0146167202289002

Barkley, R. A. (2010). *Differential diagnosis of adults with ADHD: the role of executive function and self-regulation.* Journal of Clinical Psychiatry. doi.org/10. 4088/JCP.9066tx1c.

Ashkan B., Mira-Lynn C., & Hanna C. (2020). *Emotion*

dysregulation in adults with attention deficit hyperactivity disorder: a meta-analysis. National Library of Medicine. 10.1186/s12888-020-2442-7

Whiteside, S. P., & Abramowitz, J. S. (2004). *Obsessive compulsive symptoms and expression of anger.* Cog Ther Res, 28:2, 59–68.

Bzostek, S. H., & Beck, A. N. (2011). *Familial instability and young children's physical health.* Social Science & Medicine, 73, 282–292.

Lerner, J. S., Li, Y., Valdesolo, P., & Kassam, K. S. (2015). *Emotion and decision making.* Annu. Rev. Psychol. 66, 799–823. doi: 10.1146/annurev-psych-010213-115043

Zhang, K. (2016). Fuel in the Fire: The Effects of Anger on Risky Decision Making. Doctoral dissertation, University of Konstanz, Konstanz.

Giancola, P. R., Josephs, R. A., Parrott, D. J. & Duke, A. A. (2010). *Alcohol myopia revisited: Clarifying aggression and other acts of disinhibition through a distorted lens.* Perspectives on Psychological Science, 5(3), 265-278.

Martina de Witte, Ana da Silva P., Geert-Jan S., Xavier M., Arjan E. R., & Susan van Hooren (2020). Music therapy for stress reduction: a systematic review and meta-analysis. Pages 134-159. https://doi.org/10. 1080/17437199.2020.1846580

Hussien, A. M., Silpasuwanchai, C., Salehzadeh, N. K., Ren, X. (2017). *Understanding the role of human senses in interactive meditation.* In: Proceedings of the 2017 CHI Conference on Human Factors in Computing Systems. doi:10.1145/3025453.3026000

National Institute for the Clinical Application of Behavioral Medicine (NICABM). (2017). *How anger affects your brain and body* [Online]. Accessed from https://www.iahe.com/docs/articles/nicabm-anger-infographic-printable-pdf.pdf

Witusik A., Pietras T. (2019). *Music therapy as a complementary form of therapy for mental disorders.* Pol Merkur Lekarski. 47(282):240-243.

National Center for Complementary and Integrative Health (NICCH). (2016). *Meditation: In depth. National Institutes of Health (NIH)* [Online]. Accessed from https://www.nccih.nih.gov/health/meditation-in-depth

Lykins, E. L. B., & Baer, R. (2009). *Psychological Func-*

tioning in a Sample of Long-Term Practitioners of Mindfulness Meditation [Online]. Journal of Cognitive Psychotherapy, 23(3): 226-241. Accessed from https://www.researchgate.net/publication/233512098_Psychological_Functioning_in_a_Sample_of_Long-Term_Practitioners_of_Mindfulness_Meditation

Borders, A., Jajodia, A., & Earleywine, M. (2010). *Could Mindfulness Decrease Anger, Hostility, and Aggression by Decreasing Rumination?* [Online]. Aggressive Behavior, 36(10): 28-44. Accessed from https://www.researchgate.net/publication/38031479

Askari, I. (2019). *The role of the belief system for anger management of couples with anger and aggression: A cognitive-behavioral perspective.* Journal of Rational-Emotive & Cognitive-Behavior Therapy, 37(3), 223-240. https://doi.org/10.1007/s10942-018-0307-5

Ana, B. (2020). 9 Therapist-Approved Tips for Reframing Your Existential Anxiety [Online]. Accessed from https://www.self.com/story/reframing-existential-anxiety

Cannon, M. (2011). *The Gift of Anger: Seven Steps to*

Uncover the Meaning of Anger and Gain Awareness, True Strength, and Peace. New Harbinger Publications, Inc

Tafrate, R. C., & Kassinove, H. (2019). *Anger management for everyone: Ten proven strategies to help you control anger and live a happier life.* New Harbinger Publications.

Berle D., Moulds M., & Starcevic V. (2016). *Does Emotional Reasoning Change During Cognitive Behavioural Therapy for Anxiety?* Cognitive Behaviour Therapy. doi:10.1080/16506073.2015.1115892

Printed in Great Britain
by Amazon

20343360R00120